Also by Pat Croce

I Feel Great and You Will Too!

110%

Victory Journal

LEAD

OR GET OFF THE POT!

The Seven Secrets of a Self-Made Leader

PAT CROCE

WITH BILL LYON

A FIRESIDE BOOK

Published by Simon & Schuster

New York   London   Toronto   Sydney

FIRESIDE
Rockefeller Center
1230 Avenue of the Americas
New York, NY 10020

For information about special discounts for bulk purchases,
please contact Simon & Schuster Special Sales
at 1-800-456-6798 or business@simonandschuster.com

Designed by Christine Weathersbee

Manufactured in the United States of America

10   9   8   7   6   5   4   3   2

Library of Congress Cataloging-in-Publication Data
Croce, Pat.
    Lead or get off the pot! / Pat Croce with Bill Lyon.
        p.   cm.
    1. Leadership. 2. Executive ability. 3. Success in business.
        I. Lyon, Bill. II. Title.
HD57.7.C752 2004
658.4'092—dc22   2003059509

ISBN 0-7432-4681-0

To DJ

Whose little life has been such a big lesson
of leadership and inspiration to so many.

Acknowledgments

I don't know anyone who says life is easy. But I do know that life is easier when you surround yourself with people who share in your vision with an unbridled passion, conviction, and enthusiasm. And the writing of *Lead or Get Off the Pot!* was a case in point.

I admit this book was not an easy undertaking. The reliving of my past business lives, the purging of my mistakes and mishaps, the stoking of shadows and celebrations buried deep in the recesses of my memory banks, and the chronicling of hard-earned lessons learned (using a two-finger-pecking typing method) required the unwavering assistance of several special individuals.

"Dig a little deeper here!" "Be more specific!" "I want more *Croce* in this lesson." "Does the reader feel your passion?" "Is it in-your-face enough?" "Now *this* reflects what this title is all about!" These were just a few of the love notes scribbled across my manuscript by the Caribbean Queen of Edits, Cherise Grant.

And I'm happy, now, to say the headaches she created helped make the journey worthwhile.

Lucky for me, I had the rare opportunity to work once again

with two very creative and focused friends who made this journey enjoyable. I treasure the assistance and guidance of Bill
Lyon and my personal editor, Greg Jones, without whom I
would never have elicited, let alone overcome, the Queen's
challenges.

Contents

Foreword

For many years, *Reader's Digest* had a monthly article entitled "The Most Unforgettable Character I've Ever Met." After meeting Pat Croce and spending an evening with him at the Ernst & Young Entrepreneur of the Year National Awards Gala in Palm Springs, California, I came away impressed and supercharged— he is truly an unforgettable character. Pat had just finished giving a speech to several thousand of the country's most successful entrepreneurs—all regional Entrepreneur of the Year Award winners from around the country. They responded to Pat with fire and enthusiasm, giving him the only standing ovation that had been given in the conference for years. When he told me of this book project and its title I thought, *How fitting, how appropriate.* I was impressed with how deeply he listened, that he wasn't full of himself, and that he was on a continuous growing and learning adventure himself.

In 1969, I took a sabbatical from my university teaching to write a book. Wandering through the stacks of a university library in Hawaii one day, I pulled down a book, opened it, and read three lines that truly changed my life. They became the foundation for my own work, *The 7 Habits of Highly Effective People.* Here are the lines:

Between stimulus and response there is a space.

In that space lies your freedom
and power to choose your response.

In those responses lie your growth and your happiness.

As I studied the book you are about to read, that experience and learning in Hawaii came back to me in a powerful way. I found, magnificently illustrated in this book, the capacity of a person to *observe* his own participation in life, to step in and reinvent himself, to acknowledge mistakes and not let the past hold his future hostage, and thus to learn from those mistakes and move on to new learnings and new contributions. You will feel, as you read this material, an affirmation of the space between stimulus and response in *yourself*—that you are not primarily the product of your *nature* (genes) or your *nurture* (upbringing and present environment), but the product of your *choices*. Of course, both nature and nurture influence tremendously, but they do not determine us. Our choices do.

As you read this book—from the introduction through the conclusion—you will sense how Pat made use of this space between his conditions and his decisions. You will also see how the space became larger and larger until he literally became the creative force of his own life. We are not animals who are totally a product of genes and/or training. We, like Pat, don't need to extrapolate from our past to create our future. We, too, can become the creative force of our own lives.

You will sense that the learnings Pat shares in this book are really his "earnings." In other words, he *earned* these lessons, often the hard way. Moreover, he's so authentic and so in touch with these processes of growth that, at times, you will feel you are overhearing his most intimate conversations.

Carl Rogers, the great American psychologist and one of the leaders in the field of communications theory, concluded one of his major works with the idea, "That which is most personal is most general." When Pat shares his intimate insights, I think you will *identify* with his experience and feel, as I do, that you can personalize his insights and learnings. They truly have general application. This is not an abstract theory book, but very practical, real-life, and down-to-earth. In a fundamental sense, he is teaching the basic principles of leadership: vision, team building, consistent communication, integrity, deep listening, Golden Rule service, and celebration.

One of my favorite books is *Man's Search for Meaning* by Viktor Frankl—an account of the learnings Frankl acquired in the death camps of Nazi Germany. He, too, became an observer of his own participation in life, reinvented himself, and earned his learnings. It was when he was stripped naked, tortured, and had various experiments performed on his body that he discovered this space between stimulus and response and came to realize that he could choose to find meaning in his suffering. He could learn from the adversity and prepare himself to share those learnings with others. The insights from his experiences eventually led, after his release from the death camp, to the development of one of the major forces in psychotherapy, called "logotherapy," which deals with the need for meaning in our lives. "He who has a why can live with any what and with any how."

Just as Pat's leadership reinvented the Philadelphia 76ers, *our* leadership can reinvent our own lives, our families, and the organizations to which we belong. It makes no difference what our position is. This entire book communicates that leadership is a choice, not a position, and that everyone who will "get off the pot," exercise initiative, and follow correct principles will, like a magnet, draw a passionate team toward a vision that inspires commitment and passion. In this way leadership (influence) becomes broadly distributed throughout an organization rather than being concentrated in a one-man show. This is particularly true in today's knowledge-worker age, where most of the added value to goods and services comes from knowledge workers, not manual workers.

Principles are universal, timeless, and self-evident. That is, you can't argue against them any more than you could ever build trust without trustworthiness. In this book, Pat is not telling us to follow all of the various practices that work for him but, rather, to listen to the underlying principles upon which those practices are based and then to come up with our own practices that reflect the unique realities of our own personality and our own situation.

Jim Collins, in his best-selling business book, *Good to Great*, chronicles those organizations that, over a long period of time, have gone from good to great and identifies the underlying characteristics of the leadership that brought this transformation about. He calls it "Level 5 Leadership"—a paradoxical combination of humility and fierce willpower and unending determination to make good things happen. Humility has to do with the person feeling that it isn't all about him or her but about the cause, the project, or the work—particularly the building up of other people. Fierce determination has to do with the willpower to do whatever it takes, consistent with correct principles, to further that cause or to accomplish a particular goal.

This book has the spirit of both humility and fierce determination. As you read it you will sense that you cannot violate true principles with impunity, particularly the integrity principle that is a central theme throughout the book.

Finally, let me suggest the greatest way I know to get the

most from this book: Teach it chapter by chapter to your loved ones and associates. Teaching it will enable you to legitimatize changes you seek to make in your life, including personal style changes. It will legitimatize the opportunity to apologize to others for mistakes so you can move on and free yourself of the labels people have placed on you. As you teach this material, you can discuss practical applications of it because, ultimately and in the last analysis, to really internalize the learnings, we must practice the principles in ways that are appropriate to our own situation. To know and not to do is really not to know. To learn and not to do is really not to learn. This book can be a launching pad for making significant personal and organizational changes if you will sincerely attempt to share it with your teams at home and at work. In doing so, you will feel the space between stimulus and response becoming larger and larger; you will become less a function of past programming, present circumstances, or labels that have been put on you, and you will become more the creative force of your own life and an instrument to better serve others.

—STEPHEN R. COVEY

Introduction

In everyone's life, there are major influences and defining events that help shape who—and what—you are.

A pivotal moment in my life happened on a typical Sunday afternoon when I was a boy. My mother returned from church and was beaming—not so much because of the weekly mass, but because of something that happened afterward.

As my mother made her way outside, a lady tapped her on the shoulder and asked, "Are you Mrs. Croce?" My mom answered, "Yes." The lady said that "Mr. Croce" used to be her insurance man, and explained how his generosity of spirit gave her sustenance, support, and most of all, hope, in her darkest hour. In those days, my dad would travel from door to door to collect his customers' insurance payments. Premiums were pretty low then, yet this lady found it difficult to keep up payments when her husband contracted a terminal illness that dragged on for months. After all corners had been cut, she decided to stop paying the insurance premiums. Following her husband's death, she was shocked to receive an insurance cash settlement; after all, she knew that the policy should have been canceled. Then she learned from the insurance company that my dad had continued to make the premium payments—and even triggered the payment of death benefits—without telling her. Instead of facing her twilight years not only alone, but completely broke, she would have the resources to live her final days with dignity and some measure of comfort.

Who knows why my dad did it? When my mom told us the story later that day, my dad just smiled and shrugged it off.

I may not have understood at the time, but my father's actions, in retrospect, taught me the most important lesson I've learned: You make a living by what you get, but you make a life by what you give.

We will never know the final tally of random acts of kindness performed by my father in his lifetime. But I do know this: in every way, by word and by deed, the original Pat Croce was a leader. I have tried mightily to follow in his footsteps, and in the process discovered much of what I know about leadership.

Leadership is not about getting the money or the fame or the accolades or the status. It is not about one person making decisions and giving orders from a lofty perch, pulpit, or vacuum. Leadership is not possible without a leader who genuinely cares about the cause and those behind it. Leadership is not a dictatorship, but a fellowship.

Leadership is about compassion, and hard work, and dedication, and tireless enthusiasm for what you're doing and for the people you're doing it with. A leader challenges and mediates and motivates and communicates and inspires. Sometimes with a shout, sometimes with a whisper.

And always by example.

Ironically, the month my father died, in 1993, I was putting the finishing touches on the deal to sell my Sports Physical Therapists franchise, marking the earnest beginning of my journey as a speaker and motivator. (Of course, becoming minority owner and president of the Philadelphia 76ers was on the horizon, too, though no one knew it at the time.) All of the theories and practices and ethics and ethos that I would begin to advocate with massive adrenaline had started with my father. And though he would not be there to witness the next stage of my life, his guidance and exemplary, seamless leadership would be put to great use.

I have always believed that if I can do it, so can you. And I am not afraid to tell you so. Now, in *Lead or Get Off the Pot!*, I lay out all of the concepts and systems and skill sets, as well as the overall philosophy of leadership, that I've used from the training room to the boardroom and beyond. Some of these I got from my dad. Some I learned from the many books I've read and other influences that I cherish (you'll see that I have a tendency to refer to these things often, and with great passion). And some I learned from experience—questioning, listening, reacting, erring, learning, challenging, and always growing.

These skills and this mind-set apply everywhere, from the playground to the office of the CEO, because the laws of leadership are universal. They apply to every circumstance, grade school through retirement home. And they work for everyone, from the quiet and meek to the loud and sleek. You don't have to be the top dog to stir up the pack; every dog can have his day—every day. And every man or woman, boy or girl, can develop the qualities that make a great leader, whether you're rubbing elbows with the titans of industry or the common man.

I see leadership as a bold and daring adventure, and I challenge you to attack it in the same way that I do. You don't have to tattoo a pirate ship on your forearm (like me) to express your insatiable desire to set out and conquer. But I do urge you to take every chance you can to get on the ship! Every day offers an opportunity to lead; it's up to you to grab the wheel with both hands and steer your journey toward that glittering treasure chest of dreams.

It is my hope and intent that this book will enable you to become a leader—or to become a better leader—no matter in what venture, situation, or station in life you find yourself.

LEAD
OR GET OFF
THE POT!

ONE

Paint the Vision in Vivid Colors

On July 25, 2001, the memorable day that ended my five-year tenure as president of the Philadelphia 76ers, I attended a press conference in the First Union Center packed with members of my staff, numerous friends, and media members representing every conceivable mode of communication. Following an introduction that thanked me for my enthusiasm, hard work, and leadership, I approached the podium with a smile and proudly shared the following message as part of my farewell speech:

A little over five years ago, I stated that I wanted

- to create a world-class organization,
- to empower the fans and restore their pride and passion back into the Sixers franchise,
- to use the franchise to help galvanize and have a positive effect on our communities, and
- to win a world championship.

I'm proud to say that we achieved all but one of these goals. The dream is still the parade . . . and dreams have no deadlines.

As I stepped away from the podium, there was a sadness in the air for what might have been. But there was also a reverberating buzz from the excitement we had all just shared, and for what we had in fact accomplished.

And so I walked away from the organization before realizing the final goal, but in a way, we had truly lived the dream. Though we fell just three wins shy of attaining the world championship, it wasn't for a lack of inspiration or perspiration. We were an action-oriented organization, and truly a team on and off the court. We broke franchise records in attendance, merchandise sales, and overall revenue, as well as breaking the franchise consecutive-win record, on a thrilling journey from worst to first. And it was all part of the plan.

In the 1995–96 season, the year before I joined the Sixers, the team finished in last place. They recorded eighteen wins against sixty-four losses, had an average attendance per game of 11,935 (20 percent of those tickets were "comps," or free-ticket giveaways), appeared on national television only once, and had relatively no merchandise sales.

In fact, no one wanted to wear 76ers gear for fear of looking like a loser or being associated with an embarrassing situation. It was a clear case of "out of sight, out of mind."

Five years later, in the 2000–2001 season, the team won the Atlantic Division with fifty-six wins, won the Eastern Conference championship, averaged almost twenty thousand fans per game (tripling revenues), enjoyed forty-two appearances on national TV, and became the top-selling team for merchandise, accounting for 25 percent of all NBA-licensed sales product. (Can you spell "A.I."?)

The franchise had become Philadelphia's talk of the town. And the transformation from an utter embarrassment to a city asset could never have happened without maximum effort, without a coordinated action plan, and without willing participants.

And before all of that, of course, there had to be a vision.

There's an old Japanese proverb: "Vision without action is a daydream. Action without vision is a nightmare." Either way you look at it, one without the other creates a conclusion that falls somewhere short of celebration.

This concept is shared by all great leaders, though their expression of the concept can vary as much as their personalities and personal histories. Last year, I was honored to be the keynote speaker at the 2002 Entrepreneur of the Year Awards ceremony in Palm Springs, California. It was an exciting challenge for me, having to address and inspire 2,500 of my kindred souls whose visions

> **PAT CROCE POINTER:**
>
> Vision without action is a daydream. Action without vision is a nightmare.

had fueled their actions to fruition. And later in the evening, I had the pleasure of being introduced by *The Tonight Show*'s Jay Leno as a presenter of one of the prestigious awards. I love Jay's wit and wisdom, and since I've had the opportunity to be on his top-rated show several times in the past, we had a little fun during my introduction.

But the icing on the cake was my seat in the magnificent ballroom. Front and center. Perfect sight lines. Only a whisper away from the stage. And, I was seated next to the "American Socrates" on the subject of leadership: Dr. Stephen Covey.

I had read Dr. Covey's books and related strongly to his mission and message, and so I was eager to talk shop with one of the greatest interpreters of leadership theory. He complimented me on my speech and we started into a discussion on the greatest values of leadership. He reaffirmed the importance of my concept of a leader's need to "paint the vision." In fact, he related my concept to one of his own—Habit #2 from his best-seller *The 7 Habits of Highly Effective People*. It states: "Begin with the End in Mind." Dr. Covey explained that when people do not keep the end clearly in mind, they get caught up in an activity trap, in the busy-ness of life, and end up working harder than necessary at climbing the ladder of success, only to discover that the ladder is leaning up against the wrong wall.

I couldn't agree more! Avoiding such a devastating pitfall in the end is a task that must be tackled in the beginning. It all starts with finding your vision. And finding your vision is not something that magically comes to you; it is something that you have to create out of nothing. I call this process "the Vision Quest."

THE VISION QUEST

Finding your vision in any situation, and in any station in life, is not something that can be bought, taught, learned, or stolen. It has to be created out of thin air. It is something that has to start inside you, and most of the time it's been brewing inside you for longer than you even know.

But what, exactly, is this "vision" we're talking about?

Well, we can start by defining what a leader's vision is *not*. It's not a fleeting apparition with blurry boundaries, or a faint mirage with fuzzy form. It may be a fantastic dream, but it's not an unrealistic daydream.

A leader's vision is a fusion of the goal at hand, the actions needed to reach that goal, and the attitude that must always color the campaign. It is a complex plan with a singular focused purpose.

The vision is the force behind the action. It is the underlying mantra as you strive for the goal. The vision creates cohesion within the group, and the vision makes it possible to overcome the inevitable obstacles that arise.

Because of the vision's importance, it is crucial for the leader to state the vision and preach the mission early and often.

And even though a leader's vision comes from within, it often has to be coaxed out. When you start out on any new endeavor, set out on a Vision Quest by asking yourself some questions about the state of things, such as:

- What am I passionate about?
- Does this idea fuel my passion?
- What would I do if I knew I couldn't fail?
- What opportunity is staring me in the face?
- Is there a need unfulfilled?
- How would I fill that need differently?
- Why is it done this way?
- Is there a better way?
- How will my involvement make an impact?
- *What if . . . ?*

There are plenty of other questions that can be asked, depending upon your situation; just remember that no great answers exist without great questions. When you ask Vision Quest questions like these, you begin to create possibilities. This is where your creativity and imagination can truly fly.

I've always believed that just because something always has been does not necessarily mean that it always has to be. In fact, when you simply try to maintain the status quo, you are going to fall two steps behind. That is, one step behind the person who is envisioning continuous improvement and refinement, and two steps behind the person who is already implementing such vision.

But some people are averse to change. You have probably heard their common refrain, excuse, justification: "We've always done it that way." And you probably also know that these six words are the most expensive words in the business world.

I don't understand that way of thinking. If you're not in tune with the dynamic environment you're operating within, you're going to be left out. And make no mistake about it: every human situation is dynamic and filled with the potential for change.

As Socrates said, "The unexamined life is not worth living." That applies to every aspect of your life. It's a good thing to keep your eyes open for opportunities to get more out of—or put more into—your business, relationships, hobbies, and other interests. It's not productive to continue working with things and systems that don't work, like keeping a dead-end job because it's convenient, or doing anything in life "out of habit." Staying firmly in the same old tracks will eventually grind you into a rut.

It's what they call getting "railroaded." And for good reason . . .

The U.S. standard railroad gauge—which is the distance between all railroad rails—is exactly four feet eight and one-half inches. We are not talking four or five feet. We are talking exactly four feet eight and one-half inches! Doesn't that sound like an odd number to you? Why was that inconvenient gauge used?

Because that's the way they built the rail lines in England, and it was the English expatriates who built the U.S. railroads.

So why did the English use that gauge?

Because the first rail lines were built by the same people who built the prerailroad tramways, and that's the gauge they used.

So why did they use that gauge for the tramways?

Because the people who built the tramways used the same tools and jigs that they used for building wagons, which used that specific wheel spacing.

So why did wagon builders use such odd wheel spacing?

Because that was the spacing of the wheel ruts along the roads of England, and if they used any other wheel spacing, the wagon wheels would have broken.

So who built those old rutted roads?

The ruts were made from the wheels of the Roman war chariots. Imperial Rome built the first long-distance roads in Europe for their legions as they ventured out to conquer the world.

So why did the Roman chariot makers use such odd wheel spacing?

Because the war chariots were made just wide enough to accommodate the rear ends of two warhorses.

So the next time you're confronted with a horse's ass who rationalizes, "Because we've always done it that way," you can chuckle at his ignorance. And, hopefully, take advantage of an opportunity to set your vision on greater things.

In your Vision Quest, search for the ways and means that will enable you to have a unique impact, leave an imprint, and make a difference. Listen to intelligent, innovative people whom you respect and admire. Observe the environment of the times and the daily goings-on around you. Watch the moves and countermoves of those people who travel on the road less worn. (For me, these travelers include individuals like Sir Richard Branson of Virgin Group, Brian Roberts of Comcast Corporation, Oprah Winfrey, and Jimmy Buffett, to name a few.) To this end, do what I have found to be most effective: read.

And in the course of your reading, listen to the words with a "leader's eye." A leader doesn't just see what everyone else sees; she sees what *is* as well as what *could be*. She constantly asks the question: What if? She is like a great painter who looks at a blank canvas and sees a masterpiece. And with bold, vivid strokes, she paints her vision.

THE VISION KEEPER

I recently read Peter Guber's book, *Shoot Out*, after meeting with the movie mogul in his Hollywood home and listening to his views and vision. The man has made multiple blockbuster movies, ranging from *Batman* to *Rain Man*. I was pumped to find our common ground when he spoke about "vision keepers"— what a great term! He described how influential filmmakers, writers, musicians, and innovators of all kinds use the power of imagination to galvanize and inspire. Their creative influence, he says, rallies others and mobilizes the resources needed to bring their vision to reality.

For the greatest innovators and leaders, the vision and its eventual reality are one and the same, and making dreams a reality is just a matter of time and execution. These great leaders' ability to bridge the vision and the reality so seamlessly is a tribute to the power of imagination.

One of the greatest imaginations of the twentieth century belonged to Walt Disney. My favorite Walt Disney story has nothing to do with lovable animals or animated heroes or memorable theme songs; it's a simple story that illustrates the power of the great leader's vision.

I first heard the story from Mike West, a friend of mine who is a senior producer-director for Walt Disney Imagineering at Disney World in Orlando, Florida. Mike has been with the entertainment giant for almost twenty-five years and has seen incredible advancements in both the company's entertainment centers and its film and television productions. Advancements, you might think, that Walt Disney himself could not have predicted.

Or could he have?

When Disney World opened in 1971, Walt Disney was not present to witness the grand opening of his greatest dream come true—he had died five years earlier. During the spectacular opening ceremonies, the host of the festivities introduced Walt's widow, Lillian Disney, who would say a few words on stage for the occasion.

"Mrs. Disney," the host beamed with reverence, "I wish Walt could have seen this."

Lillian stood up, walked over to the podium, adjusted the microphone, and said, "He did." And then she sat down.

That simple statement said it all.

Such stories of great innovators and vision keepers are well documented, and their wisdom is out there for the taking and integrating.

So make time to read newspapers, magazines, trade journals, newsletters, and books. Look for cutting-edge ideas that might be cut even finer. Seek out kernels of wisdom that you can tuck away for future reference. Try to find connections where there apparently aren't any. Become inspired by the risk takers and trailblazers of the world. And especially learn some lessons from others' failures.

Nowadays, nearly everyone has access to a virtually limitless library at the click of a mouse. Still, there is something special about browsing through a bookstore, handling a wide variety of titles, and paging through the volumes of information in search of the seeds of hopes and dreams that may inspire you.

Maybe it is the physicality involved—the walking, squatting, lifting, and reaching around the bookshelves—that evokes the philosophy of my buddy Euse Mita, who says that *if you want to move people emotionally, then you must move them physically.* A creative leader in the automotive industry, Euse is famous for getting the owners of auto dealerships out of their seats, followed immediately by getting their minds out of their ruts.

Personally, I love the mental stimulation that a stroll through the aisles always provides. When I travel through that world of wonder with all of its opportunities—many of which are brilliantly disguised as impossible situations—I often find myself thinking, *Wow, how did they think of that?* You never know what will flip the switch on your cerebral lightbulb, and what will stimulate you to perceive the impossible to be possible.

> **PAT CROCE POINTER:**
>
> You never know what will flip the switch on your cerebral lightbulb, and what will stimulate you to perceive the impossible to be possible.

The exercise of asking a series of Vision Quest queries worked wonders for me when I was just starting out as a staff physical therapist in 1977. I was dressed in my white lab jacket treating patients in the bowels of Tri-County Hospital in Springfield, Pennsylvania. The physical therapy department's shabby digs were not a stone's throw away from the boiler room. At the time, such low-rent real estate was not unusual for PT departments. Still, it seemed strange to me that they were always located in windowless rooms, usually in basements, that were void of the energy and bright environment conducive to feeling great.

Why is it done this way? Is there a better way? What if . . . ?

What if I took the physical therapy department outside of the hospital into a freestanding facility? What if it had windows and sunlight? What if I modeled the department to resemble the athletic training rooms seen in collegiate and professional atmospheres? Why not utilize some of the same equipment used in health clubs? Must the staff wear white lab jackets? Why not let all patients feel they are being treated like professional athletes?

With the onset of the fitness craze in the 1970s—and especially jogging, aerobic dancing, weight lifting, and Nautilus training—came an increase in the number of athletic injuries. Weekend warriors were losing the battle of the bulge and injuring themselves by the minute. In answering my own questions, I saw that a need was going unmet. I saw an opportunity staring me in the face. I saw possibilities. I saw a vision begin to develop.

After I posed a long string of questions over a period of time, the Vision Quest was complete. My vision was to create a sports medicine center combining the best of both worlds: athletic training and physical therapy. We would help people heal by making them feel great with optimum exercise and therapy offered in a bright and energetic environment. Sounds like a no-brainer today. But twenty-five years ago, the only facility resembling that of my vision was located within the confines of Temple University in Philadelphia. And that center didn't even have windows.

One year later, I opened the first sports medicine center in a hospital setting in the United States: Haverford Community Hospital Sports Medicine Center. Four years later, I opened Sports Physical Therapists, the first private non-hospital-based sports medicine center in the country. Ten years after that, we opened our fortieth center.

The "me" had become "we."

Then, in 1995, after the highly profitable sale of Sports Physical Therapists to a public company called NovaCare, my next Vision Quest began. The "we" had reverted back to "me," and I performed the exercise all over again. I watched. I listened. I learned. And of course, I read.

The switch flipped and the lightbulb flickered when I saw an article in the *Philadelphia Inquirer* describing the bright future of the National Basketball Association (NBA) in general and the value appreciation of the Philadelphia 76ers in particular, despite that team's losing record, poor attendance, and fan apathy. I remember my first thought being simply, *That's interesting.*

Fuel was added to the fire of my imagination when, browsing through the bookstore, I picked up a magazine and read a flattering profile on the marketing magic of NBA commissioner David Stern. Continuing to browse on return trips, I flipped through biographies of professional sports team owners, professional athletes, and big-time college and pro coaches, and even a book on servicing sports fans.

My interest was supremely piqued, and I became focused. I started asking myself some crazy questions. . . .

What if I was the owner of the Philadelphia 76ers? What would I do differently? How would I make an impact? Is there a better way to run this team? Is the team even for sale? What if . . . ?

It is at this precise moment—the *start* of a vision—that most people *stop.* Two lives ago, when I was the fitness guru preaching the benefits of a healthy lifestyle, I'd recite this little poem that comically defined this widespread dilemma:

> *I spent a fortune on a trampoline,*
> *A stationary bike, and a rowing machine.*

Complete with gadgets to read my pulse,
And gadgets to prove my progress results.

And others to show the miles I've charted,
But they left off the gadget to get me started.

So when I started to ask these questions about the Sixers, I knew I needed to take action on my vision . . . now! I needed to get off the pot! Sure enough, and soon enough, cursory telephone calls revealed that Harold Katz, the Sixers' owner, might in time be interested in selling the team. *Might.*

Might to me was as good as *yes!*

In less than a year, I was in the middle of a $500 million deal. And that was just the beginning.

WRITE IT DOWN . . . PLEASE!

At the beginning of any new endeavor, I'm always excited and pumped and jam-packed with energy. And because I'm a very physical person, this extra energy comes out in the way I walk and talk and carry myself. My words become animated and urgent, and my arms and legs pretty much follow suit. But beneath all the bluster on the outside, my mind is working twice as fast on the inside. At the early stage of a project, when anything is possible, that's when all the really valuable ideas crop up. They come fast and furious, and every single one of them seems like a winner. It's in this mental maelstrom that the original seed of the vision takes shape. It's your challenge to try to harness all that energy, to capture all those ideas like lightning in a bottle.

And there's only one thing you'll need to do this: a pen. Or a pencil. Or even a crayon.

When the ideas start to come, scribble them down. It doesn't matter where or on what. It doesn't matter what color. And it doesn't matter what your penmanship looks like—well, as long as you can understand it. Because what matters is that you capture the idea at the moment of inception so that you don't miss a future moment of opportunity.

I'm a fanatic about jotting down ideas and things to do on anything within my reach—pieces of newspaper, napkins, backs of business cards—or methodically posting them into my handheld electronic organizer. Once they're written down, I can focus my attention on the issue at hand instead of wasting precious energy trying to prevent my mind from forgetting something important.

Flowers for the wife . . . oops! Phone call on an employee's birthday . . . oops, another missed opportunity. A special gift related to a client's passion . . . but what was that passion again? A new idea to vault your company past the competition . . . damn, where did that idea go?

The time invested in writing down an idea or errand is time well spent. I'll be damned, but deals do die, promises are broken, sales are stolen, love is lost, and opportunities will vanish while you wait or wonder what happened to that great or small *something* that you meant to do.

How many times have you heard yourself say, "I should have

> **PAT CROCE POINTER:**
>
> Deals do die, promises are broken, sales are stolen, love is lost, and opportunities will vanish while you wait or wonder what happened to that great or small *something* that you meant to do.
>
>

done this" or "I should have done that"? Because you didn't write it down, you forgot to do it or say it, and now you smell like *should.*

Don't smell like *should. Should* stinks. Wipe the *should* off yourself. Slap the *should* out of yourself. Of course, we all know that *should* happens, but don't let it happen to you. Write it down!

During staff meetings, I always enjoyed telling stories to drive home a specific point. For example:

An elderly couple had been married a long time and had come to the twilight of their journey, yet they continued to appreciate all that happened along the way. Alas, their good intentions were overpowered by memory loss that was becoming increasingly severe. It concerned them enough that they finally decided they'd best consult their physician.

He examined them and found everything pretty much the way it's supposed to be when your odometer has turned over.

"Nothing to be terribly concerned about," he told them. "We reach a certain age and we forget things. It's a fact of life. Maybe not an especially pleasant one, but it's pretty much unavoidable. But if it will help, you might want to write reminders to yourself. Little forget-me-not notes."

The couple returned home, and that night after dinner retired to the den to read and watch TV. They didn't need to say all that much. As with couples that have been together for about as long as they can, uh, remember, they were quite comfortable with silence.

Finally, the woman said: "I'm in the mood for some ice cream."

And she started out of her chair.

"No, no, sit there," the husband said. "I was planning on going to the kitchen myself. I'll bring back your ice cream."

"Well, that's very thoughtful, dear. I appreciate it. But remember what the doctor suggested? Perhaps you'd better write yourself a little reminder."

The husband reddened in anger. "Good grief, woman, I'm only going to the kitchen, not New York. And I can surely remember something as simple as a bowl of ice cream."

The wife frowned. "All right, but I'd really like some strawberries on the ice cream." Gently, almost in a whisper, she added: "Maybe you'd better write it down, like the doctor suggested."

The husband flared and snorted: "A bowl of ice cream . . . with strawberries . . . I got it. It's not like I have to recite the Gettysburg Address."

And the wife, ever so carefully, said: "You know how fond I am of whipped cream. I'd love to have some whipped cream on top of the strawberries and ice cream. So probably you should go ahead and write . . ."

The husband drew himself upright into a tower of seething outrage and stomped out of the room, toward the kitchen, muttering and fussing as he went, and over his shoulder he said: "Okay, woman, I'm off to the North Pole, and I'll return with your bowl of ice cream with the strawberries and the whipped cream, and then we'll see who can remember her name and who can't."

He was gone quite a time.

Five minutes. Then ten. Fifteen.

Finally, he emerged from the kitchen in triumph and vindication. He was bearing a large tray, which he set down with a grand flourish in front of his wife. On it was a platter of bacon and eggs, the bacon still making sizzling noises and giving off that irresistible aroma, and the eggs meticulously prepared and begging to have a fork burst the yolk from them.

The husband stepped back and awaited the apology and the applause that he was sure were his just due.

The woman looked curiously at the platter of bacon and eggs. And then she looked up at her husband and asked, simply: "So where's the toast?"

Obviously, the blame for this gastronomic gaffe could be placed squarely on the kindly gentleman's advanced age. But when it comes to precious ideas and brilliant flashes of thought, such gems can be lost by anyone who tries to commit them to memory rather than paper. No matter what your age.

When you have a great thought, or even when you think of a simple task that needs doing, write it down!

Make a to-do list. And when you complete a task, check that item off and move on to the next significant step of your action plan. Each check mark represents a tiny victory, a sense of accomplishment, a step in the right direction. And it prevents you from losing ground and wasting time trying to remember what was so important that you were supposed to do.

A Chinese philosopher once said: "The weakest ink is better than the strongest mind."

THE VISION BREAKDOWN

Once your vision is clear, but before you take any action, it is essential to construct what I call a "Vision Breakdown." The term itself seems to imply that your view is impaired or that something is in need of repair. But actually, just the opposite is true.

The Vision Breakdown enables you to see your future more clearly and to build up a solid foundation for success. It is a road map that will take you from the Point A of your vision to the Point B of your goals. In the simplest of terms, the Vision Breakdown is a to-do list, albeit a lengthy, complex, and ever-growing one.

But don't let that last statement discourage you. Because,

mostly, drafting a Vision Breakdown is fun, exciting, and rife with sweet anticipation.

It consists of three simple steps, plus one not-so-simple step:

1. With your vision in front of you, work backward and break it down into a series of time-sensitive goals. Since goals are more defined than the vision, you should be able to paint a vivid picture of them . . . with borders.

   When I took over the Sixers, for example, the vision was to reestablish franchise pride, profitability, and production. Those are real things, yet they exist in the realm of mind more than of matter.

   The goals, on the other hand, included signing the best players possible immediately, establishing a winning record within two years, and claiming the NBA championship within five years.

2. Next, take those goals and break each one down even further into a series of necessary tasks. Tasks are the major to-do aspects of your game plan; they are clearly defined projects of limited duration.

   Continuing with the Sixers model, one of our goals was to fill our roster with the best possible players. So we had to set forth tasks designed to fulfill that goal, such as enhancing the computerized systems of the team's scouting, increasing the number of scouts covering the country, and expanding our relationships with players' agents.

3. Then, take the tasks and break them down even further into finite action steps. Action steps are the nuts-and-bolts items that fill your daily to-do lists. These lists should be *prioritized* to enhance progress.

   When prioritizing your action steps, remember the 3-D approach:

Do it now! Don't wait. Don't procrastinate. Many action steps are first and foremost *timely* and should be scheduled at the top of your to-do list, requiring immediate action.

Delegate it. Get more done more efficiently by assigning action steps to responsible individuals on your team.

Defer it. Meanwhile, some action steps are not in the urgent category and can be planned for a later date. Deferred items go to the bottom of your to-do list.

Completing the Sixers model, to support our scouting activities we immediately checked off action steps by visiting scouting combines in Phoenix and Chicago, where potential NBA draft picks would be put through their drills and skills testing.

4. Now here's the not-so-simple step. In fact, it is quite difficult. Are you ready? You must actually get off the pot and take action!

All this vision development and goal setting and prioritizing of action steps looks wonderful on paper. But until you actually make a physical move and take action—that is, pick up the phone, call the travel agent, and book a flight to Phoenix with a change of clothes and a second flight to Chicago—all the dreaming and scheming in the world will get you nowhere near your vision.

Being a fan and collector of pirate lore, I saved this little poem from a *Bits & Pieces* publication that seems appropriate at the moment:

Desire is the treasure map.
Knowledge is the treasure chest.
Wisdom is the jewel.
But they all stay buried without action.

WHOSE CHOICE IS IT ANYWAY?

One of the most important words in the English language, relative to creating your vision and taking action, is *choice.*

Throughout your journey from vision to celebration, from the goals to the goalposts, you'll be faced with a myriad of choices, starting in earnest with the first action step. And along the way, your choices will range from the easy and effortless to the tough and extremely painful. But it is important to remember, as you come to every new fork in the road, that each choice carries significance and creates the world you live in. You do not live by chance; you live by choice. As one of my favorite little poems states so perfectly:

There's a choice you have to make in everything you do;
and always keep in mind, the choice you make, makes you.

You can choose to smile or wear a frown, speak up or stay down, join the crowd in futile complaint or enact positive change, take the path less worn or fall into the path with the well-worn rut. But whatever you do, it's your choice. There is no "have to" in this journey of life. You don't "have to" do anything . . . nothing, nada, zip, zilch. You can either choose to do it or you can choose the consequences.

For example, you can choose to adhere to my Service Commandment #6: Be Prompt and Professional, and be true to your commitments in a punctual manner, *or* you can choose to potentially be labeled discourteous, disrespectful, undisciplined, lazy, or rude. On a lighter note, guys can choose to lower the toilet seat at home, *or* they can choose the possibility of sleeping on the couch!

Of course, there will be times when you don't choose your circumstances. "Shit happens" to everyone—like breaking your leg in a motorcycle accident. But even when it does, you still have a choice: you can always choose your attitude. It's not what happens to you, but what happens *within* you, that matters.

Too often we choose to do something—or nothing—out of habit or because of peer pressure. We react automatically and without conscious thought of the consequences. But choices shouldn't be wasted or made in haste. Think of each choice as an opportunity, and you will make them carefully and strategically with a focus on your vision.

Of course, you can't make every decision. It is vitally important to delegate authority and allow other key individuals the freedom to make choices that, hopefully, further the game plan more effectively, more efficiently, and more happily. And when you have succeeded in creating and imparting a strong vision, others have a greater chance to consistently make the right decisions.

Responsibility, however, remains solely yours. You can delegate authority and decision making, but you can never delegate responsibility. As the vision lives in your mind, the responsibility rests squarely on your head. And so you'd better convince the others to hold the vision close to their hearts.

> **PAT CROCE POINTER:**
>
> You can delegate authority and decision making, but you can never delegate responsibility. As the vision lives in your mind, the responsibility rests squarely on your head.

OH NO! THE FRED INCIDENT

A great way to reaffirm the vision to others is to illustrate it by example, and through your own actions and critical choices.

One of the first memorable decisions I had to make as president of the Philadelphia 76ers was in response to an irate season-ticket holder weeks after I took over the reins.

Just prior to my arrival, season-ticket-plan invoices for the upcoming 1996–97 season had been mailed out to season-ticket holders. Even though they numbered fewer than three thousand, these customers represented a core group of passionate basketball fans, provided important revenue, and were the only base we had on which to grow.

Unbeknownst to me, these invoices included a "deposit" due date that fans had to meet in order to reserve their seats. These deposit payments on their season tickets were nonrefundable.

The nonrefundable deposit was not the problem. The problem came to my attention when longtime season-ticket holder Fred Lavner voiced his displeasure with the response he had received from the ticket-box manager regarding his concern.

Fred was perplexed by how we could confiscate his money and/or threaten him with the loss of his treasured seats if he did not pay the deposit by the due date, when neither he nor anyone in the organization knew if there would be an increase in ticket prices for the upcoming season!

I talked to Fred, listened to his concerns, and appreciated his position. And since no one provides you with an owner's manual when you own and operate a professional sports team, I relied on another manual: the Golden Rule.

What would I do if I were in Fred's shoes? What would I want my team to do for me, a dedicated fan? These questions ultimately helped make my choice very easy, although there were several choices from which to choose in the first place.

I could have chosen to avoid contact with the customer, thus supporting the delegated decision made by my ticket-box manager. I could have chosen to parrot the normal operating procedures to the customer: "Blah, blah, blah . . . see you—and your money—at the game." I could have chosen to eliminate the season-ticket deposit altogether. Or I could have chosen to maintain the policy of requesting a deposit to ensure the same seat assignment, but eliminate the nonrefundable clause.

PAT CROCE POINTER:

Managers do things right; leaders do the right thing.

Ultimately, I chose the latter and I decided that all deposits would be refundable until the team made decisions for the upcoming season regarding ticket prices, season-ticket discounts, arena seating structure, parking costs, and a host of other issues that I never knew existed.

The "Fred Incident" provided a perfect opportunity for me to communicate to my new staff the distinction between managers and leaders: Managers do things right; leaders do the right thing. And I wanted and needed and expected *leaders*. No others need apply.

After all, effective management without successful leadership is like straightening the deck chairs on the *Titanic*.

Yes, the ticket-box manager was maintaining the status quo and following normal operating procedures in the correct way. But "maintaining" and "status quo" and "normal" were words that would not be appreciated or tolerated by the new president.

Meanwhile, the Sixers made a fan for life and Fred made a friend for life. During the five years of my tenure as president, Fred felt compelled to become my personal Ralph Nader, ensuring that my choices were made with the utmost care and understanding.

In other words, he was a pain in the ass! But a welcomed and needed pain in the ass.

76ERS VISION BREAKDOWN

Once the acquisition of the 76ers was complete, and the vision of its potential defined, I set out on a Vision Breakdown in order to create a strategic blueprint for success. No detail would be spared, and no thought would be left off my to-do list. The Vision Breakdown developed over a brief and brisk period of time, and continued to develop even after I began taking action. Here is the exact model that was used to launch the resurrection and revitalization of the 76ers organization.

VISION: Reestablish franchise pride, profitability, and production.

GOAL: Create a world-class organization.

Task: Interview and build a passionate management team.

Action Step: Call my longtime secretary, Sue Barbacane, to offer new executive assistant position.

Action Step: Call Dave Coskey and offer VP of marketing position.

Action Step: Schedule appointment with John Lucas to discuss his present GM–head coach position.

Task: Evaluate the workplace environment.

Action Step: Tour the franchise offices at Veterans Stadium.

Action Step: Visit the team's training facility and evaluate amenities.

Action Step: Schedule meeting with CoreStates Center's president, Peter Luukko, to tour new locker room and office space.

Task: Adjust the financial budget to coincide with my new direction.

Action Step: Schedule meeting with controller Andy Speiser.

Action Step: Review arena seat allocations and ticket-pricing schedule.

Action Step: Examine vendor list and advertising sales allocations.

Task: Survey the staff, vendors, and customers/fans.

Action Step: Schedule appointment with each existing team employee.

Action Step: Schedule a vendor luncheon.

Action Step: Schedule a private lunch with sportswriters.

> 1. *Philadelphia Inquirer*'s Bill Lyon
> 2. *Philadelphia Daily News*'s Phil Jasner
> 3. *USA Today*'s Greg Boeck

Action Step: Organize a meeting with season-ticket holders prior to the start of 1996–97 season.

Task: Examine the franchise's sales and service standards.

Action Step: Schedule sales team meeting with sales staff.

Action Step: Schedule meeting with ticket-box manager.

Action Step: Make phantom phone calls to sales and ticket-box staff to monitor responses to ticket purchasing and customer complaints.

Action Step: Distribute "Ten Commandments of Customer Service."

Task: Create a commitment to community initiatives.

Action Step: Expand community relations department.

Action Step: Speak at community and chamber events.

Action Step: Develop at least a half-dozen community initiatives (Sixers Slam Dunk Diabetes, Sixers Neighborhood Basketball League, Catholic Youth Organization Sports Tribute, Project HOME, Read for Ronald, Sixers Summer Hoops Tour).

Task: Permit the fans accessibility to the team via lines of communication.

Action Step: Create a fan relations department.

Action Step: Evaluate public relations firms.

Action Step: Issue press releases on all team developments.

Action Step: Respond to all calls and correspondence.
1. Telephone log
2. E-mail and snail-mail log

Task: Develop a positive, exciting, entertaining
              brand.

Action Step: Schedule a meeting with NBA Entertainment president Adam Silver.

Action Step: Create marketing and advertising plan parameters.

Action Step: Order new staff shirts adding black color to logo.

Action Step: Call NBA to change logo design.

Action Step: Create new arena floor design and color scheme.

Action Step: Interview TV and radio game announcers.

Action Step: Change game times to accommodate families.

Action Step: Visit WIP 610 sports radio station.

Action Step: Develop ingredients for the game's "Show."

    1. PA announcer

    2. Dance team coordinator

    3. Mascot tryouts

    4. House band members

    5. Video components of scoreboard Jumbotron

    6. Arena music coordinator

Goal: Win the NBA championship.

Task: Create relationships within the NBA
              organization.

Action Step: Schedule visit to Commissioner David Stern's office.

Action Step: Become an active member of NBA's board of governors.

Action Step: Volunteer for NBA committees.

Task: Call and visit NBA winning teams for their protocols.

Action Step: Steal, borrow, and buy necessary services and ideas.

Action Step: Call NBA team executives for advice.

1. Pat Williams, Orlando Magic
2. Jerry Coangelo, Phoenix Suns
3. Stan Kastin, Atlanta Hawks
4. Jerry West, L.A. Lakers
5. John Nash, Washington Bullets

Action Step: Visit and tour franchises.

1. Chicago
2. Orlando
3. Phoenix
4. New York

Task: Evaluate the team's scouting talent and systems.

Action Step: Interview staff and organizational structure.

Action Step: Compare computer systems with winning teams' protocols.

Action Step: Visit scouting combines.

1. Phoenix
2. Chicago

Task: Review team personnel and financial
                   obligations.

Action Step: Meet with team "capologist" Andy
Speiser.

Action Step: Contact NBA for player salary and term
comparisons.

Action Step: Meet with each player.

    1. Schedule dinner with Jerry Stackhouse
      in Philadelphia, Pennsylvania.

    2. Meet Allen Iverson in Newport News, Vir-
      ginia.

    3. Visit Derrick Coleman in Detroit, Michigan.

Task: Learn the NBA policies and procedures.

Action Step: Read *NBA Official Guide* and *NBA Register.*

Action Step: Schedule meeting with team's beat
writers.

Action Step: Call players' agents and create agent log.

TWO

Build a *Passionate* Team

After you have envisioned the dream and planned the scheme, the focus turns to building a *passionate* team.

I'm not necessarily talking about the nuts and bolts of actually building a team—i.e., hiring, job training, and other human resources duties—although some of these concepts are touched on here. Rather, this chapter is about the constant infusion of passion and enthusiasm that a leader must mete out.

Whether you're building from the ground up or inheriting a group that's already together, the first and foremost quality you need to uphold is passion. Find out what drives the people around you, and foster those needs. And by all means, wear your own passion on your sleeve, and let it rub off on others.

The seed of success starts inside you and spreads to your team of two, and then it grows from there. The moment "me" changes to "we" is the genesis of your adventure to fulfill your vision.

When I began to see real definition and cohesion in my 76ers Vision Breakdown—a fusion of the vision, goals, tasks, and action steps—it was time to start physically making some moves to turn the vision into reality. And my very first move involved picking up the telephone and calling my longtime secretary, Sue Barbacane, to ask if she would be interested in helping me resurrect the Philadelphia 76ers franchise. Initially, there was stone-cold silence on the other end of the line. That, I found out later, was not hesitation but rather shock and subdued excitement. The subdued excitement did not last long.

Sue replied, "Of course I would! When do we start?"

Her passion was music to my ears.

It has been said that a leader looks for his vision first, and then his people; and that people look for a leader first, and then his or her vision. This dynamic is the foundation of team chemistry. The leader is the combustible catalyst, and the rest of the team provides the daily spark that sets the vision into explosive motion.

One of the essential secrets to my success has been my ability to build a passionate team. And I mean light-your-pants-on-fire passionate. I believe I hit grand slams with the creation of Sports Physical Therapists and the resurgence of the Philadelphia 76ers organization because in both instances I started out with a hit . . . and then another hit . . . and another hit . . . until the bases were loaded with enthusiastic, talented employees.

Each of those hits became a "score" because I was fortunate enough to hire the right person for the position. Through each individual's unyielding passion for his work, his ability to share his knowledge and experience, his steadfast commitment to our shared vision, and his willingness to work together cohesively and consistently like a championship unit must, we became a team on a mission. The mission was the realization of our goals and dream.

There is a lot of truth in the premise that success starts at the top. But there is no top if there is no team. So you start recruiting players, employees, staff, partners, assistants, aides, and others, with an eye toward their attitude, assets, and ambition. Getting the right people is crucial because the transition from "me" to "we" is a scary prospect.

I remember vividly when the "we" occurred in both of my most significant past business lives. It was at the precise moment when someone other than myself would be representing me. It's frightening to think that another person will now speak for you in word and deed. Will she be able to capture your energy level? Will she embrace and translate your vision? Will she use the right words and actions? Will she *care* as much as you do?

When someone proves to be the wrong choice, you've lessened your chances of achieving your goals. But when personnel choices make a perfect fit, the sky's the limit—for immediate gain and for the long term as well. It's an intense responsibility. But the process can be a tremendous amount of fun, too. And the potential rewards are beyond your imagination.

As noted, this chapter is not so much about *building* a team as it is about building a *passionate* team. I've always had help from professional personnel directors and department heads for the former responsibility; whereas the latter responsibility was and is mostly mine. It's the leader's job to carry passion like a torch, and to consistently pass that torch to every member of the team.

TRIPLE A:
ATTITUDE, ASSETS,
AND AMBITION

From my very first employee, I was always in search of a team of doers. Not talkers. Not dreamers. Not pretenders. I wanted contenders!

And I instinctively knew that the onus was on me to find those who fit the bill. Leaders, of course, have lots of onuses. This particular one happens to be comprehensive and never-ending. It's comprehensive because you must evaluate every aspect of those you choose to work with. And it's never-ending because you must reevaluate these evaluations regularly . . . without fail!

Did I mention entertaining, enlightening, and rewarding? Evaluating and maintaining an awareness of your staff is all these things, too. It takes lots of listening and inquiring, and requires an underlying sense of caring. Ultimately, what I always look for in my evaluations is a person's attitude, assets, and ambition.

> **PAT CROCE POINTER:**
>
> From my very first employee, I was always in search of a team of doers. Not talkers. Not dreamers. Not pretenders. I wanted contenders!

1. Attitude

Thomas Edison said that genius is 99 percent perspiration and 1 percent inspiration.

To me, success is 100 percent attitude! Because your attitude affects the goals you set, informs your work ethic, influences your ability to overcome obstacles, and creates the foundation from which all your thoughts and actions grow.

And it's contagious.

I've always believed in the philosophy that success comes in "cans" and failure comes in "can'ts."

Here is a poem of anonymous origin—known to all who have ever worked for me—that illustrates this astounding fact:

> *The ones who miss all the fun*
> *Are those who say, "It can't be done."*

In solemn pride they stand aloof
And greet each venture with reproof.
Had they the power they'd efface
The history of the human race.
We'd have no radio or motor cars,
No street lit by electric stars,
No telegraph nor telephone,
We'd linger in the age of stone.
The world would sleep if things were run
By those who say, "It can't be done."

I prefer to associate with people who love the world to be wide-awake! I want individuals who will throw off their covers, wipe the sleep from their minds, slap their hands together, and embrace the day. I want those who truly believe: *It's going to be a great day!* Every day!

I look for this quality when I am putting together a winning team, and I reinforce it on a daily basis.

I heard a story once that left an indelible mark on my hiring process. Years ago, a brand-new Holiday Inn was preparing to launch, and management had scheduled a full day of interviewing candidates to fill the numerous positions open on the new staff.

The hotel's general manager instructed his department heads—who were to perform the interviews—to automatically eliminate anyone who didn't smile within the first five seconds.

No teeth showing, then get the hell out of here!

I've adopted and practiced a similar policy ever since.

When I interviewed Lisa Schramm for a secretary position in 1978, the "smile policy" was in full effect. (Lisa is now Lisa Pennacchia, since she married my vice president of marketing, Ray Pennacchia. I told you that the team has to be cohesive!) I remember Lisa entering my office wearing a bright and beautiful smile. Right then and there, I mentally checked off the "attitude" category of my evaluation prerequisites.

Lisa had the 5-second rule beat by 4.9 seconds. In fact, over the course of ten years, Lisa set the record for smiles and for customer satisfaction. Her joyous exuberance coupled with her natural smarts and efficient attention to detail made her an MVP employee. Such visible and visceral passion is contagious in a couple of ways: it rubs off on every task you undertake, and it rubs off on all of the people you interact with each and every day.

Clearly, those people who bring passion to their position are invaluable.

Having passion for your job—and for the journey of life, for that matter—begins with a positive, optimistic attitude. A consistently upbeat temperament makes those you work with try a little harder and care a little more. It adds a sense of confidence to every contact you make and every project you undertake. And it stimulates a willingness to embrace change, seek new ideas, and seize opportunities.

And when you are in a leadership position with the responsibility to build a passionate team, why would you increase your burden of stress by having to tolerate a negative individual throughout the course of the workday, every day?

As far as I'm concerned, no leader should. We spend too much time at work, so why not attempt to make it as pleasant as possible?

Life is too damn short!

There is a universal saying in sports that states, "Players with a good attitude don't guarantee a success, but players with a bad attitude guarantee a failure."

I've seen this saying come to life. And it's not a pretty sight.

I want and need people who look at the world, like me, through rose-colored glasses. (In fact, my glasses are literally rose-colored!)

And so, in the ongoing process of evaluating and maintaining assistance in any venture (business, community, charity, or play), attitude spends more time in my spotlight than any other variable. Attitude is easy to assess, and it has a direct correlation to success.

Bad attitude . . . bon voyage!

At times and in all fields, individuals are recruited because their assets and talents apparently offset their bad attitude.

But not by me!

Throughout my twenty-one years in professional sports (fifteen years in the training room, five years in the boardroom, and one year in the NBC Sports studio room), I have never seen a highly talented player with a bad attitude lift a team to championship status.

Conversely, I have witnessed players with equivalent talent, combined with a great attitude and a focused ambition, help their team to be the best in the business.

We all have witnessed the magic when great assets, attitude, and ambition unite in one person and at one time. (Make that six times.) Do the initials M.J. sound familiar?

Thump . . . thump . . . thump . . .

The arena was empty, so there was nothing to muffle the sound of the basketball bouncing on hardwood. So regular was the cadence, the rhythm of the sound, that it became musical.

And sure enough, there was a maestro, and he was rehearsing. But instead of a tuxedo, he was wearing baggy sweats and sneakers. Instead of a baton, he was conducting with a basketball. And making sweet music.

Maestro Michael Jeffrey Jordan, walker-on-air, was practicing before an audience of three—two janitors and a curious eavesdropper. Myself.

It was more than three hours before game time, and here was the greatest basketball player of all time, by himself, fifteen feet from the basket, shooting free throws. Bouncing the ball, shooting . . . bouncing the ball, shooting . . . over and over and over in an endless syncopation.

Why would M.J., of all people, be out there putting in overtime?

The answer to that question is short and sweet. It's because he *wants* to be the greatest, because he loves and enjoys his craft, and because his strong positive attitude urges him always to strive to get even better.

Thump . . . thump . . . thump . . .

Up close, I could see Michael Jordan furrowing his brow in concentration while shooting his practice free throws, draining one after another. And then I noticed something else—he was shooting with his eyes *shut!*

He has even been known to shoot free throws in a game with his eyes shut. He'll wink at an opponent, pull the shades down, and release a shot that is soft as cotton. Most of the time, it goes down. And it takes the other team's heart with it.

Talk about demoralizing your opponent; that kind of gamesmanship can psychologically destroy him. And it takes a sharply honed positive attitude to pull off such a feat.

"Hey, I'll beat you without looking." Or, "I'll take you on blindfolded."

Such a gambit requires a considerable ego, a staggering amount of self-confidence, and more than a little swagger. But to pull it off mostly requires attitude and the assets of skill and focus. And for everyone, even M.J., these things take time and commitment to develop.

Michael made the progression from beginner to star to leader in the most dramatic of manners. And yes, he was a star before he was a leader.

In team sports, the ultimate measurement of your value as a leader comes down to two questions: Do you make all those around you better? And are you able to combine their diverse and disparate talents and personalities into a cohesive unit?

Answering these questions is a two-step process. First you must lead by example, putting in time and making sacrifices that put you in the position to win. Then you must convince others around you to sublimate their own needs for the good of the common cause.

Michael Jordan was spectacularly successful in these respects. He won three consecutive NBA championships with a supporting cast that, with the exception of Scottie Pippen, was ordinary at best. After a fling with professional baseball, he returned to the NBA and, with another unremarkable group, won three more in a row.

> ## PAT CROCE POINTER:
>
> In team sports, the ultimate measurement of your value as a leader comes down to two questions: Do you make all those around you better? And are you able to combine their diverse and disparate talents and personalities into a cohesive unit?
>
>

M.J. is a living example of the adage "Individuals play the game but teams win championships." He couldn't do it alone, and neither can you. Success requires the commitment of a team of individuals whose personal goals converge with your vision's goals. And behind it all, there has to be an edge. A character. An attitude.

2. Assets

Every employee has unique assets. He also has the potential to expand these skills, and to acquire new ones. It is each person's responsibility to make the most of his abilities. And it is the leader's job to provide the tools needed to maximize individual assets while removing the obstacles that would minimize them.

Each team member's assets need to be defined and filed, then regularly referred to—and sometimes even deferred to. They should be treated like natural resources, and used to maximum impact.

When a new person joins my passionate team, as far as I'm concerned she has limitless potential. I find out what her best abilities are and then immediately put those to use. As her participation grows, I assess development of known strengths and talents while seeking opportunities to utilize the person in other ways. In the best-case scenario, someone's newly acquired strengths and skills become very obvious as she strives to emphasize her eagerness and ability to grow.

Sometimes, though, being good at one role doesn't necessarily translate into being good at another. And a leader must be willing to take this risk when a quality person begins to step up and stand out.

One of my staff physical therapists was so good with her patients and the other members of the staff—and was so consistently willing to accept additional responsibilities—that I earmarked her for a manager's role as our SPT centers began to expand.

It was a risk, since Debbie Kuebler's experience did not overwhelmingly suggest that she could handle the position. As a staff physical therapist, she was responsible only for one-on-one interaction with her patients and their referring physicians. As a

manager and the center's leader, she would have roles and responsibilities that encompassed others' actions, too. Of course,
it turns out that Debbie was more than ready to attack the job,
and she proved that growth and new challenges were clearly
within her scope.

Not only did Debbie effectively manage an SPT center, but
when we needed someone to help expand the SPT culture and
policies and procedures into our centers in the Midwest, she
packed her bags and made the move. Her leadership skill set
continued to improve, and she went on to become an all-star
district manager.

Eventually, Debbie left us to accept even greater responsibilities with another team. . . .

Her husband, Alan Lindabery, stole her away to create a
family of four gorgeous daughters!

I'm just glad that she was part of our family for a time. I'm
also glad that, in the end, Debbie's personal dream came true
and she got exactly what she had always aspired to have.

3. Ambition

On my passionate team, there is never room for the traditional
"team player." To me, that expression describes someone who is
looking for all the answers from others; who is always willing to
follow the majority without question; who is quick to defer to others; who performs his role only; who is afraid to take chances on
hunches or cutting-edge ideas; and who does not have a winning
instinct.

There was one occasion when, because I made a sponta-
neous judgment call instead of following a prescribed procedure, I was accused of not being a team player. First, I was taken
aback. Shocked, in fact! Then, after a moment of silent
thought, I said, "Thanks." Because if being a team player meant

staying in line and playing follow the slow-moving leader, then not being a traditional team player was a compliment to me.

This incident occurred during my two-year stint at Nova-Care following its acquisition of SPT. During that time, I helped inculcate our passionate culture into the entire organization, especially into the acquisition of new centers that were being absorbed on a regular basis.

I took the new role personally. And any time I received notice that physicians were complaining of less-than-top-shelf service, or when staff turnover was becoming a problem, I would fly to the center or centers in question (with one or two members of my special quality hit team in tow) and attack the problem . . . immediately!

Unfortunately, it seems that corporate protocol required my obtaining the finance department's approval for all expenses in advance, which I understood and appreciated. However, if "advance" meant waiting in line for the in-bin to empty, resulting in the chance of losing either business or good team members, then get out of my way! Get off the pot!

I like when someone flashes a little ambition. It shows he's hungry. It reveals his belief that something personal is at stake here—whatever the endeavor may be. And when someone takes personal interest in his job, his effort and results will increase dramatically.

This is not to say that I promote disloyalty, backbiting, or blood competition among my staff. Just the opposite is true. I see my staff as a band of rogues, working together toward a common goal, with each individual striving to be the very best in his role. The twist is that being the best includes in large measure helping those around you to be their best.

Like Mike, I want everyone on my team to *want* to succeed, both for personal interests and for the common interest. I want each individual to be vigilant in searching for ways to improve her own stature, improving the group and taking us all that much closer to our goal in the process. With each member contributing in this way, the avenues for success increase and widen exponentially.

As bands of pirates would constantly remind each other, "No prey, no pay."

My team members must always be on the lookout for what's best for them—their "prey." Then they need to attack their goals with clear action steps mixed with a touch of reckless abandon and unbridled passion. And if their head is in the right place, their best interest will be in *our* best interest.

When I interview people and investigate the state of employees' minds and hearts, I make a note of their ambitions and dreams. I encourage them to have personal goals that fit within the overall vision, and I support their efforts to achieve them. Often I learn things that surprise—not to mention satisfy—me.

When I first met with Billy King, for example, I did not intend to make him the general manager of the Sixers. (I had hired a rookie general manager the prior year, and I publicly ate the entire crow for it.) Coach Larry Brown had recommended that I evaluate Billy for the position of director of basketball operations. On the strength of Coach Brown's recommendation, I brought Billy in for a conversation. I wanted to see what he was thinking and craving and dreaming.

PAT CROCE POINTER:

They need to attack their goals with clear action steps mixed with a touch of reckless abandon and unbridled passion. And if their head is in the right place, their best interest will be in *our* best interest.

Within the first hour of our first sit-down conversation, I asked this simple question:

"If this pen was a magic wand," I said, holding up my Pilot pen, "and you could create for yourself the perfect job, what would it be?"

Billy didn't hesitate. He looked directly at me, and calmly, with great assurance, gave his answer: "I would want to be governor."

"Governor?" I laughed aloud.

But I loved it! This guy clearly had great ambition mixed with unmitigated conviction.

During our second meeting, Billy threw me another ambitious curveball. He said that he wasn't concerned with the salary. . . . Just allow him to prove himself and he believed he would earn my respect and the opportunity to fill the role of general manager—and the perks that came with the position.

Smart guy! I wasn't even considering him for that position until he mentioned it! But through the course of all our conversations, and with the full support and endorsement of Larry Brown, that is exactly the position to which Billy King was appointed after only one year of passionate, intelligent service.

Over the next couple of years, my evaluation of Billy King's passion, ambition, and confidence proved to be no fluke. He played a major part in building the team that went to the NBA Finals during my final year in 2001.

I hope one day he runs for governor of Pennsylvania!

DELEGATION BUILT A NATION OF FORTY

The only way to grow is to delegate. And the only way to delegate is with conviction and follow-up.

Delegating important responsibilities creates a deep sense of trust, offers a significant and exciting opportunity for personal growth, and puts you as a group in a position to expand greatly.

Of course, delegating important duties is like taking a leap of faith. You don't know if an individual will be a competent success or a complete failure. But if your evaluation of his attitude, assets, and ambition was on the mark, then you will probably be in for a pleasant surprise.

Still, be prepared to struggle with the process, especially the first time you go from "me" to "we."

The most intense delegation of responsibilities (but not ultimate responsibility) I've ever faced came when I reached my first plateau of success—establishing my first franchise. Though it was a difficult decision, I made it, and I was determined to live with it. Some years later, I was able to look back at that particular plateau from much loftier heights to see that my leap of faith had paid off.

Big time!

Just one year after my first Sports Physical Therapists center opened in Broomall, Pennsylvania, I was advised by a number of local doctors that another center might prosper in nearby Ridley Township.

In my mind, I was already successful. I had achieved my vision of starting an independent physical therapy center (outside the traditional hospital setting), and the reality of my mission statement had exceeded expectations. With the doctors' proposal in mind, though, I started seriously to consider expansion. I just didn't know what form it was going to take. Should I expand the square footage of the existing center, or open a completely new second center?

My business manager, Steve Mountain, was the first person in my own camp to second the notion. And knowing that I could either expand the square footage of one center or expand the business by opening a second one, "Mountain-man" strongly urged me to open the second center. He even suggested the perfect person to run it:

Ed "Fast Eddie" Miersch, one of my top staffers at SPT.

I knew Fast Eddie very well, and I had a tremendous amount of respect for his wisdom, work ethic, passion, and commitment. What I didn't have was the comfort level to allow me to release control of my own business (and my reputation) into another's hands.

Yet I did have faith in both Eddie's will and skills and Mountain-man's endorsement of him. Over the course of several weeks, I recounted many of the challenges and accomplishments we had faced and achieved together. And whenever we met to discuss the possibilities, they talked and I listened. In the end, the fact that they were so energized by this new challenge gave me the emotional energy that I needed to complement the practical information that had already met my standards.

I went for it. And Fast Eddie nailed it.

The Ridley center was a resounding success, and Fast Eddie managed to maintain and promote the original vision of SPT to my complete satisfaction and to his own great benefit.

Forty franchises later, Sports Physical Therapists was a major national success under Fast Eddie's continued direction and Mountain-man's sure, steady counsel. Meanwhile, I had placed major responsibility into many others' hands. And though things didn't always run perfectly, I always tried to respect the authority and choices that I had delegated and given to others.

SLOGANS DON'T GUARANTEE SUCCESS

Sometimes, after you've handed over a particular duty, you momentarily find yourself wishing that you hadn't done so. You may think: *I could have done that so much better myself! Why did I let someone else handle such an important job? What was I thinking?*

It is in these times that you have to dip deeper into your well of trust and give your delegate some more slack. Of course you should continue to monitor the situation—as you should monitor all aspects of your business—but don't be so quick to judge and condemn. Sometimes an encouraging word from the leader at a time when criticism may be expected can go a long way to ensuring eventual success.

It's vitally important to extend praise when an idea doesn't work. Praise pays. And if you praise only the efforts that win and always demean the efforts that lose, you practically destroy any opportunity that the individual might have had to hit a home run in the future.

Our first marketing campaign for the Sixers' season in 1996–97 was centered around the tag line "It's Not Just a Game . . . It's a Revolution."

Sounds like a strong slogan, doesn't it. Puts you in the mind of righteous action, us-against-the-world teamwork, and the sound of blaring guns.

Well . . . it backfired!

That season really was a revolution.

> **PAT CROCE POINTER:**
>
> If you praise only the efforts that win and always demean the efforts that lose, you practically destroy any opportunity that the individual might have had to hit a home run in the future.

There was new ownership, new vision, a new attitude, and a new star in Allen Iverson. But when the wins didn't materialize as fast as the fans expected, the media had a field day, with headlines like "The Revolution Is Revolting" and "The Sixers Are Losing the Revolution" and "Pat Croce Shot Himself in the Foot."

But I praised Dave Coskey and Lara Price—my marketing gurus in charge of the campaign—along with their entire marketing team for successfully creating a buzz. If nothing else, the city definitely knew of our campaign, even though it may have been embarrassing at times.

Still, that first stray shot of the revolution—which clearly missed its mark—would not go for naught. Eventually, Dave and Lara went back to the drawing board and transformed the campaign to include several other tag lines over the following four years that hit their mark right on the bull's-eye . . . every time!

The next season, our campaign read: "All Business . . . All Fun!" A secondary slogan said: "When It Comes to Business, We Are All Fun!" This was the season that Larry Brown was hired to head the basketball team, and his business approach to the game made the game more fun because it led to even more wins.

In the 1998–99 season, the Sixers rocked the city with the slogan "This House Is Rockin'," and we enjoyed our first winning season in almost a decade. It was also the first time the Sixers had made the NBA playoffs in eight years.

Dave and Lara built on the winning momentum in 1999–2000, choosing the song "Ain't No Stopping Us Now (The Sixers Are on the Move!)" to lead our way. And we even had the original singers of McFadden and Whitehead perform the altered song for the campaign.

By 2000–2001, the dynamic marketing duo decided simply to blast their message to the fans, as if they didn't know it already: "You Gotta Be Here!"

And those fans came in record-breaking numbers to see their team advance all the way to the NBA Finals against the world champion Los Angeles Lakers.

I dread to think what would have happened with the creativity and passion of my key team members if I had chastised them for the backfire of the "Revolution" slogan. A lack of support from the top more than likely would have altered their thinking, diminished some of their passion, encouraging them to play it safe instead of throwing caution to the wind and making a statement and an impact.

Good thing I kept my mouth shut—except to extend some unexpected support at the darkest hour.

WHAT ABOUT CHAPLAIN BOB?

What happens when you just can't keep your mouth shut? What happens when you delegate a duty to a capable other, but then muddy the waters with your own tinkering?

Call it overexcitement. Call it unchecked passion. Call it what you will. But there have been times when my zeal for a particular project blinded my better judgment and caused me to undermine the authority I had delegated to a capable other.

I remember one particular gaffe that I made when I was president of the 76ers. It was a decision on a relatively simple matter, but when other people are involved, it's never simple!

I was sitting in my office in the bowels of the First Union Center about an hour before game time when Lara Price, having been promoted to vice president of marketing, knocked on the open door. She had a forlorn look on her pretty face.

"I have a concern about our national anthem singer this evening," she said.

I didn't know whom we had scheduled to sing the national anthem, but I did know we always had someone good. Our fans had enjoyed the sounds of Grover Washington Jr., Teddy Pendergrass, Boyz II Men, Patti LaBelle, Bruce Hornsby with Branford Marsalis, *The Tonight Show*'s Kevin Eubanks, and the rapper Bow Wow, to a name a few.

Tonight it was to be a fifty-three-year-old man named Bob who sang some gospel in his church, and according to Lara, his rehearsal on the court was awful. Coaches from both teams, who were with the players during the pregame shoot-around, jokingly complained to her, "You've got to be kidding. Where did you get this guy?"

Which was my exact question, since all the anthem and half-time acts had to submit video- and audiotapes for evaluation. I wondered for a second who had dropped the ball on this responsibility. . . .

It just so happened, Lara reminded me, that this guy came from me!

Some months earlier, while I was doing a radio interview at WIP (Philadelphia's popular sports station), the crazy host, Angelo Cataldi, had this ordained minister surprise me with a live, on-air audition!

A couple of bars of "The Star-Spangled Banner" sounded okay to me, and so as a courtesy to Angelo—and feeling sorry for the minister—I asked Lara to schedule him. I checked it off my to-do list and then I forgot about him.

Problem was, I did not ask or expect Lara to subject Bob to the strict standards that she always followed when scheduling national anthem performers. Instead, she trusted my judgment and booked Bob on the spot.

After her briefing of the rehearsal debacle, Lara and I hurried through the back of the arena to the dressing room with the star on the door. My goal was to prevent this poor guy with the rich aspirations from receiving a volcanic boo from the twenty thousand fans in attendance, including Bill Cosby sitting in the front row. This was definitely no church assembly—these were our passionate Philly sports fans. Remember, these are the same fans who received notorious national attention for booing Santa Claus at an Eagles game!

I knocked. Bob opened the door standing in his boxer shorts, white shirt, and bow tie. I told him to put his pants on because we had to talk.

Once he was dressed, I told Bob that his rehearsal wasn't so good and that his voice was all over the place. It appeared that all the bravado he'd displayed in the radio studio had been reduced to fear.

"Relax," I said. I handed him a pencil in lieu of a microphone and told him to sing as if he were standing in church—not too loud, but I still wanted to hear his passion.

"Relax a little bit more," I said. "That's good. That's good! You'll do great!"

As I was leaving, I asked, "Bob, do you have a nickname?"

"When I call into WIP radio," he replied, "they call me Chaplain Bob."

"Well, Chaplain Bob, it's great to have you kicking off our game tonight, and I've got a good feeling that we'll both be winners," I said as I glanced at the star's black tails hanging proudly by the door.

Upon returning to my office, I told Lara, "He'll be okay. But I want you to have him introduced as 'WIP's famous Chaplain Bob.' Because just in case he's off, the crazies who listen to WIP will support him, and there's a good chance the rest of the fans won't boo a chaplain."

Game time. The lights dimmed, the spotlight focused at center court, Chaplain Bob's image was magnified on the giant scoreboard, and several of us held our collective breath.

He was wonderful! He was soulful throughout, and he hit the high notes at the end of the anthem to thunderous applause. I watched as he exited the court through a gauntlet of high fives and thumbs-up, and finally as he enjoyed a huge hug from his wife.

And oh yes, we won the game.

Lara felt relieved, and so did I. My support for her was reinforced. And she had the rare opportunity to tell her boss that he had made a mistake! I should have asked her to evaluate Chaplain Bob, in deference to both her duty and her expertise. Oops. I'm sorry.

Luckily, I learned from this mistake. And Lara learned the benefit of sharing a few choice words of praise with Chaplain Bob.

GOALS, ROLES, AND TOLLS

Why do people work?

To make money? To make a difference? To accept challenges? To accomplish goals? To utilize their unique gifts? To earn recognition? To have fun?

For the people who work with me, I would hope that all of these reasons apply.

Whatever you are leading—whether it's a company, a civic group, a volunteer organization, a sports team, or any other band of rogues—it's important to understand the motivations of your people. And you'll find that it is invaluable to stroke these motivations early and often.

Every individual comes to the table with his or her own goals in mind. And for every goal within your vision, there are roles for various team members to fill. And for every role that's filled, there are tolls that must be paid.

The leader is in the unique position to understand the responsibilities of the group and to ensure that each individual is properly compensated.

But by "compensated," I am not talking only about money. Not by a long shot.

Sure, money is important, and it is therefore important for the leader to evaluate that aspect of the compensation package. But money is not all that matters when building a passionate team. The leader must be fully aware of the goals, roles, and tolls that affect each member of the staff. Knowing these things will lead to proper action, and effective interaction.

PAT CROCE POINTER:

The leader must be fully aware of the goals, roles, and tolls that affect each member of the staff. Knowing these things will lead to proper action, and effective interaction.

Goals. As you know, individuals come to the table with their own goals in mind and their own standards already set in place. But upon joining a team, they must assimilate the goals that are based on the overall vision that everyone is striving toward. The effective leader will work with individuals to help them understand these goals and to create an atmosphere in which they will be most reachable. And whenever a leader accommodates a connection between personal goals and the goals of the team, the individual's commitment is bound to intensify. Conversely, the benefit to the organization is greater.

Roles. Everyone has a role on a team, in a company, or in any other group situation. Usually an individual joins a group with a role in mind, and he or she begins with a specific set of duties based on that role. But it's a dynamic world, and a confident leader will consistently look for opportunities to revise and/or expand particular roles. Not that a consistent role is a bad thing—every company needs to build corporate memory via those individuals who maintain the same basic position for years. But it's important to regularly appraise the roles that exist, the people who hold them, the utilization of human resources, and the performance delivered by each role player.

Tolls. Each role includes a number of tolls that must be paid in order to accomplish the goals at hand. From time, effort, and commitment . . . to overtime, extra effort, and complete dedication, each team member will be charged with the responsibility to pay these tolls with enthusiasm and an allegiance to the vision. An astute leader will never take these tolls for granted, but rather will be aware of them and will appreciate the people paying them. It is this appreciation—which must come from the top down—that forms the ultimate two-pronged structure of compensation: recognition and remuneration.

R AND R ON THE ROCKS

"R and R" in my world doesn't mean "rest and relaxation."

Sure, everyone wants holidays and vacation days to recharge their batteries and enjoy a little fun in the sun. But that personal time can occur only periodically throughout the year. Within the framework of my passionate team, R and R means "recognition and remuneration." And it is given regularly, on the basis of merit.

The R and R structure that I have always relied on encompasses all aspects of compensation—money, time, recognition, acknowledgment, and respect.

For example, during my tenure as CEO of SPT, at the suggestion of staff members, we regularly supplemented the staff's paid benefit days with earned "wellness" days. These special days off with pay were granted based on an accumulation of consecutive workdays without calling in sick or being tardy for work. The philosophy was simple: why should staff members be penalized for never using their sick days? They shouldn't, so they would receive paid time off (PTO). For every six months of work with excellent attendance, each employee was granted one wellness day.

Health insurance, life and disability insurance, and various fringe benefits are an important part of any employee package and should be considered a vital part of the compensation plan. But when it comes to the R of remuneration, "money talks and bullshit walks," as the saying goes. First of all, it must be understood that people don't always appreciate the cost factor in a total employee benefits plan. In general, they want to see the amount of greenbacks their paycheck will bring every two weeks.

And if a cash bonus lands in their palm at any time of the year—Christmas, birthdays, anniversaries, and awards—all the better. Or how about a gift certificate for a dinner for two? Or one month of free parking? Or a small token of appreciation based on position or personality?

This is a where the R of remuneration begins to cross over to the other R—that of recognition. Every leader should look for reasons and moments to recognize members of his or her team for outstanding performance, or for increased performance, or even for par performance.

That's right. Even par performance should be recognized from time to time.

Not that you should be satisfied with par performance at *any* time. The reason for recognizing (I didn't say "rewarding") a par performer is to alert that employee to his weaknesses and subsequently set him on a path to rectify the situation. The result, hopefully, will be that he will then strive toward increased performance.

This is a good opportunity to consider the "80-20 Rule." The 80-20 Rule states that 80 percent of the work is accomplished by 20 percent of the people. In this model, the 80 percent group consists of your par performers. And this is okay; not everyone can be Michael Jordan. But when you focus on helping these par performers achieve just a little bit more, you find that your group will be achieving goals above and beyond expectations. By getting each par performer to increase productivity in small increments—urging this 80 percent group to do 30 percent of the work, say—you can lift the overall productivity beyond 100 percent efficiency to a level that I can live with: 110 percent!

> **PAT CROCE POINTER:**
>
> Every leader should look for reasons and moments to recognize members of his or her team for outstanding performance, or for increased performance, or even for par performance.

I don't expect or require the 80 percent group to do extraordinary work. But with a little recognition and encouragement, I am hoping that they can perform ordinary work extraordinarily well.

Another key aspect of granting recognition is to do it in public whenever possible.

Even though I'm a big believer in the power of handwritten, personalized congratulatory notes, I also believe that when there is a chance to share the moment of someone's success with his or her peers . . . then the leader must jump on it.

At the end of every week, my vice president of sales for the Sixers, Fran Cassidy, would summon all of the sales staff together to acknowledge the person who had sold the most full-season equivalents. (The sale of one full-season ticket is equal to one FSE. The sale of two twenty-one-game plans is equal to one FSE. And the same goes for seven six-game plans.)

In our first year with the Sixers, we started our sales and marketing campaign with a base of only 5,576 FSEs—and only 2,902 of those were full-season-ticket holders. That was a scary starting point. Obviously, we had a tough sell on our hands. In addition to selling our new vision, the sales staff was selling hope, optimism, and the resurrection of a franchise. So every sale, even a six-game-plan sale, was regarded as news to celebrate.

On Friday afternoons, Fran would move a chair to the middle of the sales pen, and following a drumroll, he would read aloud the name of the salesperson of the week. The star salesperson would approach Fran, who would hand the person a Beanie Baby in the form of a shark. Upon taking shark in hand, the salesperson would then step up onto the stool to be toasted by the sales team.

The Shark of the Week was crowned!

And since the Shark never wanted to give up the shark the following week, he or she would work even harder to keep the honor. And others would work even harder to wangle the honor away!

In addition, Fran would provide me with the names and numbers of sales-per-category for the week in his Five-Fifteen report (see chapter 5, "Listen with a Leader's Eye") so that I might write a personal note of congratulations if I was unable to attend the shark ceremony.

My three rules for praise are: Make it **personal, punctual,** and **public.**

I'm not a believer in the cookie-cutter types of congratulations cards where the boss's name is blandly signed at the bottom (most likely forged by his or her secretary), without any indication of sincerity or true acknowledgment. Notes of praise should be personalized to whom, from whom, and with a touch of heartfelt praise.

Another praise technique that I have always enjoyed as much as the beneficiaries have is the **sixty-second salute.** It's simple. For one full minute, deliver praise to a worthy individual describing *why* you appreciate her work. Defining and describing the *why* of your congratulations and adulations gives the person a sense that you actually care about, understand, and appreciate her efforts. And since no two individuals are alike and their approach to their goals may be as different as their fingerprints, the treatment is best when tailored to their personality or to the achievement being saluted.

Also, praise should always be delivered in as timely a way as possible. Just like a birthday wish loses its luster a week after the special day, so too does a heaping of praise lose a bit of its meaning when presented long after the fact.

If I was so important, then why didn't he call or write me when I won?

Speaking of birthdays, these are opportunities built especially for making individuals feel important. Birthdays are momentous occasions. Birthdays are the one unique day of the year when Santa Claus comes to one special person's door only. And one of the greatest gifts you can give is appreciation.

We all have childhood memories of our birthday parties, presents, and adventures that marked a special year. So why not add to your staff's photo album of memories a little festivity on their behalf?

Free lunch. Beautiful flowers waiting on their desk. A half day of work . . . with pay.

Every birthday should be celebrated. Those silly birthday hats never lose their magic!

TEAM BUILDING'S DIRTY DOZEN

Building a passionate team is a monumental task that requires a significant investment of time, talent, and energy. But ultimately, it pays awesome dividends.

Here's a checklist of a dozen concepts that I often refer to as a means of keeping the team-building process sharp and sure. These theories and practices have helped me immeasurably in all of my businesses, community initiatives, and other ventures. See how they work for you.

1. Praise in public and criticize in private.
2. Be more curious and less critical. Ask why and how as opposed to ranting about what should have been done. An eager ear provides greater benefits than a tart tongue.
3. Pull and don't push. To lead you must get out in front. And you must lead by pulling, not pushing. Consider an exercise that I often use to illustrate this point: I take off my belt and hand the end to a staff member while I continue to hold the buckle. When I push the buckle at the employee, nothing happens. However, when I pull the belt by the buckle, the employee follows me.

   Napoleon was asked after his stunning victory in Italy

how he made his army cross the snowcapped Alps. He replied: "One does not make a French army cross the Alps; one leads it."

4. Check your integrity. A recent study reported that only 47 percent of American employees saw the leaders of their companies as people of high personal integrity. And that was before the Enron, Arthur Andersen, Global Crossing, HealthSouth, and WorldCom scandals, among others, came to light. How can you build a passionate team to strive toward your vision when the members of the team don't trust you? You can't!

5. Foster positive emotions. One of the leader's vital jobs is to make people feel good. This is especially true during the bad times, the hard times, the down times. Do your best to help individuals deal with negative emotions and to stimulate positive emotions. Generally, people work smarter and harder when they feel good. And it's a known fact that a company's success follows the emotional climate of the team.

6. Strive to understand others. Realize that people don't leave their feelings at home when they come to work, and that it's almost impossible not to bring the stress of work into the home. Something as simple as listening to your employee's grief over a sick pet can create a positive work experience out of a lost cause.

7. Show confidence in people. A good way to motivate individuals is to ask them for their help—*I really value your opinion and input; can you help me?* This demonstrates your faith in their ability and competence, and stimulates them to work to be worthy of your concern. Not to mention that you might learn something valuable.

8. Promote charity. I like to promote team spirit by urging my employees to join together to support a cause or charity. One of the many community initiatives that we created as a Sixers franchise was the "Sixers Slam Dunk Diabetes Carnival," which was held annually at the First Union Center and involved everyone in the organization, from the top to the team itself. We recruited the input and creativity of the entire staff in order to create a memorable afternoon of fun and games, including a celebrity auction and photo and autograph opportunities. Beneath all the smiles was an awareness that we were raising funds for the Juvenile Diabetes Foundation through simple teamwork. As individuals, we knew that it would be impossible to match the synergy, creativity, and energy level of the team approach.

   As I mentioned in the introduction, I learned that you make a living by what you get but you make a life by what you give. Well, I also learned the mantra "It's not what you gain, but what you give, that truly measures the net worth of the life you live."

9. Celebrate diversity. For a leader, it's imperative to never forget that your team is a collection of individuals with different backgrounds, cultures, styles, ambitions, and needs. These differences require your use of subtle changes in approach in order to motivate the group on an individual level. One person may kick it up a notch when a challenge is tossed in her direction, whereas someone else may be threatened by that approach. Some people love a direct challenge; others do not. Remember the 80-20 Rule. A leader must find out what people's motivational buttons are. Know your staff's tendencies, then act accordingly.

10. Unleash potential. Team success hinges on your success in tapping into the potential of each and every member of the team. As Dr. Stephen Covey notes in his book *The 7 Habits of Highly Effective People,* an individual's potential can be quantified by assessing his character (who he is as a person) and his competence (what he can do). The success comes when you can make the best use of each person's time and talent. Meanwhile, they will be sharing in the commitment to accomplish your vision.

11. Set the tone. I have always attempted to create an environment of infectious enthusiasm where the expectation of excellence permeates every facet of the business. I enable, encourage, and reward individuals to help maximize their creativity and talent and provide them with a great sense of self-worth. Let the passion, compassion, intensity, and enthusiasm drip from your sleeves.

12. C.A.R.E. Above all else, you must truly care about the people with whom you work each day. There's no faking it. Here's a quick mnemonic device to keep this notion close at hand:

Compromise: Make concessions to ensure participation.
Apologize: When you are wrong, take the blame and
  say you are sorry.
Recognize: Learn from the failures and celebrate the
  successes; give compliments!
Empathize: Be genuinely concerned with your staff's
  feelings and circumstances.

As Dale Carnegie said: "You can make more friends in two months by becoming interested in other people than you can in two years by trying to get other people interested in you."

THREE

Preach the Mission . . . from Every Mountaintop

The fate of any vision rises and falls on the shoulders of its leader. And the impact a leader may have on that fate depends a great deal on his or her ability to communicate the mission loud and clear . . . and often.

What good is it to paint a vivid vision if you don't communicate it in full color and with great detail to those who would help you achieve it? Painting the vision is only the first step. Translating and instilling it into the minds and hearts of your team is what gives it life.

You can't expect people to buy into or get anything out of a mission they don't fully understand. But you *can* control the flow of communication to ensure that no ambiguity exists in anyone's mind at any time throughout the course of your quest. And you can have a lot of fun with it along the journey.

I always do.

To me, preaching the mission doesn't have to be all about robotically laying out a prescribed strategy (although laying out a strategy can be a good thing). And it doesn't have to be about stodgily scripting some official and boring document (although putting the mission in writing isn't a bad idea).

To me, preaching the mission is about you, the vision keeper, speaking your dreams and vision out loud. It's about defining who and what you are. It's about delivering a practical message with a whole lot of emotion, energy, and enthusiasm. And it's about sharing this process with those who would share the vision with you.

Constantly!

Preaching the mission must be a dynamic process, and an unending one. Most important, like all effective communication, it must also be a two-way street. As much as you state goals and dictate responsibilities, you also need to answer questions and listen to concerns and suggestions.

If you can communicate your dreams and goals so succinctly and so vividly that those around you can see them, touch them, and taste them with the same passion that you do, then fate will surely be in your favor.

> **PAT CROCE POINTER:**
>
> Preaching the mission is about you, the vision keeper, speaking your dreams and vision out loud. It's about defining who and what you are. It's about delivering a practical message with a whole lot of emotion, energy, and enthusiasm.
>
>

AN EQUILATERAL ATTACK

Your vision comes alive when you paint your dream for all to see. And your mission materializes when you add the ingredients of pride, passion, meaning, and strategy to the selling of your vision.

Think of your mission—whether it's establishing a company or organizing a successful fund-raising drive—with the same intensity as one would a military operation or a devout personal calling in life. Then let that intensity show in your words, in your body language, and in your overall demeanor. It's that sort of zealous attitude in pursuing your cause that compels people to stop and listen . . . and to follow.

I preach the message of my mission with the same fervor that I attack my fitness program—with an unyielding determination. I know that—as with fitness—if you rest, you rust. It's a constant battle to ensure that the message is spreading and that your vision's gospel is regularly read.

In all of my business and other ventures, there has always been a strong and consistent philosophical foundation upon which I have communicated the mission at hand. It starts with the Golden Rule and expands to include a trilateral approach. It's not a complicated formula, and it doesn't exist as a detailed multipage document. In fact, it's as simple as ABC . . . or more appropriately, QPF.

Quality. Profit. Fun.

I like to think of my standard mission statement as an equilateral triangle, with all three sides of the triangle being of equal length. Each of the three sides is represented by one of three words: *quality*, *profit*, and *fun*. The equal sides depict equal emphases on these concepts, with no one side or goal receiving disproportionately more emphasis than either of the other two goals.

I *always* want to ensure the highest-quality product or service: the best in the business. No shortcuts!

I want to make money: the more, the merrier. Share the profits!

And I want to have fun: a ton of fun. Life's too damn short!

The essence of the equilateral-triangle approach is that no one goal is more deserving of my team's attention than the others. I don't want to sacrifice quality to make more money. Nor do I want to have fun in lieu of ensuring the best quality. And I'll be damned if I am going to miss out on having fun by torturing my team in order to make more profit!

Every one of my employees knows my vision. They know our goals. They know their roles and duties en route to those goals. And they know all about the equilateral triangle.

Obviously, it's not too hard to memorize the three words that constitute my triangular mission statement. But, admittedly, applying the meaning of the magical triangle can become a bit murky at times. Still, any gray-area issue or endeavor can almost always be easily clarified with a few quick questions:

> *Do you believe in your ability to achieve it?*
> *Does it meet the requirements of all three goals*
>   *of our mission statement?*
> *Does it ensure the best quality?*
> *Does it enhance our profit margin?*
> *And will we have fun in the process?*

Sometimes, of course, it's necessary (not to mention wise) to sacrifice short-term results for long-term gains. But the ultimate test is whether such a sacrifice, in the end, still fulfills the three main mission requirements.

For example, an investment today for a new high-quality piece of equipment might not benefit this month's cash flow, but in time the investment would pay off handsomely in new business and an enhanced reputation.

In our Sports Physical Therapists centers, I was fanatical about keeping the facilities in pristine appearance. I didn't think

twice when incurring the expense of painting walls and replac-
ing carpet to ensure the best appearance for the patients' physical therapy experience. And I didn't count the costs when it
came to celebrating the success of our centers.

One time in the early years, when the quarterly budget for
patient revenue was surpassed, I had a U-Haul truck back up to
the center in Broomall and unload color television sets for every
employee. It was time to have a little fun, and spend a little
profit, after doing such a great job.

This rather unconventional "message" sure helped to communicate the *fun* aspect of our mission in full color! In other
terms, leaders can use more than words to communicate the
mission.

THE STRONGEST MUSCLE

A good friend of mine, Dr. Nick DiNubile, is a team physician for the Philadelphia 76ers. One night we found ourselves sitting together in the Sixers' training room, trying to calm our
nerves. It was moments before Game 7 of the 2001 NBA division
finals against Vince Carter and the Toronto Raptors, and we were
pumping ourselves up for the contest.

"Pat, what do you think is the human body's strongest
muscle? And you only get one guess." Since Dr. Nick is a de-
voted fitness nut like myself, I knew he was tossing me a
loaded question.

I thought that *he* thought that I might guess a muscle in either the back or the legs was the strongest muscle. But I decided
not to go with my gut, and I replied, "The heart!"

I knew that our two-pound muscle machine pumps almost
two thousand gallons of blood through sixty-two thousand miles
of blood vessels one hundred thousand times a day, so its

strength and importance can't be questioned. And anyone with a broken heart knows how painful that affliction can be.

I thought I had him.

"No," he replied. "Wrong answer."

"So what is it? The back?" I asked quickly.

"No. It's the tongue."

"What?" I asked skeptically.

"Just think of what the tongue can do," he said.

Suddenly I knew where he was going with his question. The tongue can cut down a person immediately, regardless of size and strength. And it can lift a person up with little effort. In fact, it can lift an entire team of people up.

> **PAT CROCE POINTER:**
>
> All great leaders share a common, underlying trait when it comes to verbal communication: they are willing to do it.
>
>

Then Dr. Nick put everything in perspective when he sat on the edge of a treatment table, said nothing, and just motioned for me to listen with him. The only voice you could hear breaking the silence of the brightly lit training room was that of Coach Larry Brown in the adjacent locker room. There, in that tense space, moments before the biggest game of the year to date, Coach Brown was motivating his players.

A leader's greatest tool, bar none, is the word.

The ability to direct, influence, and, of course, *lead* a team of people, with little more than words, is a formidable strength. Some do it with carefully chosen language; others, with infectious energy. Some rely on their overpowering voice; others use a soft-sell approach.

But all great leaders share a common, underlying trait when it comes to verbal communication: they are willing to do it.

Those who shy away from preaching the mission—because they lack preparation, are indecisive, fear failure, fear public speaking, or whatever—put that mission at risk.

A leader must be willing to speak up and communicate the message with a passion. He must be willing to state his ideas, views, and opinions in a clear, concise manner. And he must be willing to repeat the vision aloud over and over and over again.

Of course, not every leader boasts excellent public-speaking skills. If your skills are somewhat questionable, there is no question what you need to do: practice until you reach perfection (or at lease a close facsimile thereof!).

I consider myself naturally subpar in the area of public speaking. This confession may sound odd when you consider that I receive hundreds of invitations (and commissions) annually to speak at everything from high school assemblies to high-powered gatherings of Fortune 500 executives, and that the reviews my speaking engagements receive are consistently excellent. The reason I am able to overcome my natural limitations is fourfold: I do extensive preparation, play up my strengths, understand my limitations, and constantly work to overcome them. Because I am so animated, I always make sure to communicate *in person* when I need to deliver an important message. Also, I have learned that I must commit a speech to memory in order to deliver it with maximum effect and emotion.

If you struggle in this area of communication, a little understanding and effort will go a long way toward increasing your confidence and effectiveness as a speaker.

Yet every leader need not have the silver tongue of Oprah, the lofty thoughts of Lincoln, or the towering presence of Churchill to be effective. There are almost as many successful speaking styles as there are leaders.

You got where you are in large part because of the things

you have communicated verbally. Now just remember this: a couple extra decibels, a dose of passion, a pinch of body language, and the perfectly chosen words never hurt a message.

As Lee Iacocca said: "You can have brilliant ideas, but if you can't get them across, your ideas won't get you anywhere."

A LEATHERY NEGOTIATION

I learned the art of communication, and the power it wields, from my father.

Oh, I'm not speaking of the skills needed to mesmerize a vast assembly. Rather, the original Pat Croce taught me the sort of speaking a leader is apt to be called upon to do virtually every day. The kind of speaking that leaves no doubt, and yet is also diplomatic.

When I was in high school, my father took me on a trip down to South Street in Philadelphia. Nowadays, South Street is a hip, happening hot spot for people of all ages to shop, eat, dance, and drink—it's one of Philly's most popular entertainment destinations.

But in those days, it was an area to be approached cautiously, and preferably only in the bright light of day. Storefronts tended to be either boarded up or covered in charcoal and ashes. Those stores that were open for business had no costly overhead to worry about, so to speak.

There were rumors that the, uh, "suppliers" came by their wares by means that were not conventional in the usual course of commerce. Meanwhile, many storefronts featured a multi-talented employee—a combination lookout, bouncer, greeter, and insistent tour guide—who provided the perfect first impression. Invariably, this was a very large person with ears that appeared to have been chewed on by assorted animals and a nose that had been broken more times than there are fingers on a fist.

One of the stores featured this sign: SHOPLIFTERS WILL BE SHOT. There was nothing at all to suggest that this clear, concise sign was intended to be humorous.

My father was in the market for a leather coat, a midlength jacket in black, and so into one of these emporiums we strode, nodding at the barker manning the door. He was definitely someone you wanted on your side.

I think the place was called Big Al's.

And it was crammed with men's clothes, racks upon racks, the inventory stretching from floor to ceiling. Our tour guide escorted us to the back, and then up a flight of rickety stairs that creaked and groaned and emitted little puffs of dust at each footfall. I was certain we were doomed.

The second floor was packed with winter coats and jackets. The overseer was a salesman whose style and speech were as slick as his greased-back black hair. You took one look at him and automatically reached for your wallet, to make sure it was still there.

My dad spotted a jacket that was exactly what he had in mind. He tried it on. The fit was perfect. He looked approvingly in the mirror. And then he spoke.

"How much?"

"Only one hundred dollars," the salesman purred.

"How much," my dad purred right back, "for a special customer?"

The salesman smiled. The game was on. He put his arm around my father's shoulder, as though they were long-lost buddies. He leaned in conspiratorially, and whispered: "For you . . . ninety dollars."

My father looked over at me and, very slowly, very deliberately, gave me a big wink. "I'll give you fifty bucks," he told the salesman.

I swear I heard a low groan of disapproval—kind of like a sick lion with a hacking cough. The sound came from our first-floor tour guide, the gentleman with the gnawed ears and the meandering nose.

The salesman tried out his entire oily repertoire on my father, all the double talk and the fast talk, all the come-ons. He was shrewd and sly. He could have made a living dealing three-card monte on the street corner. And who knows . . . he probably did.

But my father knew all the tricks, too. For every offer and slightly reduced counteroffer, my father had the same consistent response: "Fifty bucks."

Now the salesman sighed, deeply, as though he had been mortally wounded. "Okay, just for you . . . because I like you . . . it's yours and yours alone . . . for . . . eighty-five dollars." The man smiled a sad little smile that said, *You've won—I surrender.*

And my father looked at me and said simply "Let's go, Pat."

I got his message loud and clear and followed him over to those gnarly stairs. As far as I was concerned, we couldn't get out of this joint fast enough. Mr. Bent Nose was making that sound again.

My father had one foot on the top step when the salesman dropped his act and said, "All right, my best price is seventy-five dollars."

My dad stopped, drew his foot back off the stair, turned, and walked up to the salesman. He looked him dead in the eyes and said: "Because I like you, I'll give you sixty dollars for it." And before the salesman could respond, my dad added with a courteous smile, "That's sixty dollars more than you had a minute ago."

His math was correct. His logic was impeccable.

And the salesman, being nobody's fool, understood that bargains sometimes work both ways.

I still have pictures of my dad wearing that stylish midlength black leather jacket. He looked really cool in it.

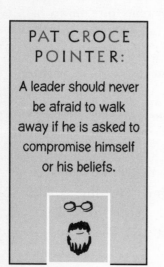

PAT CROCE POINTER:

A leader should never be afraid to walk away if he is asked to compromise himself or his beliefs.

I learned a lot from him about the power of words, about how you should set and define your goals, communicate them aloud, and then go after them with single-minded determination. I learned you should never be afraid to speak up, and should stand behind your words. I learned the value of speaking directly, without equivocation, so that there is never any doubt about what you are saying.

I learned never to presume or assume, never to think something was impossible just because somebody said it was, and that just because a thing had never been done did not mean that it couldn't be done. . . . All it meant was that you could be the first to do it.

I learned from my dad his favorite saying: "If you never ask, then the answer is always no."

Also, I learned that a leader should never be afraid to walk away if he is asked to compromise himself or his beliefs.

And, oh yes, a good leader makes sure that everyone feels like a winner when the deal is done. Burned bridges can be as dangerous to walk across as climbing those stairs at Big Al's.

I FOUND SIX Cs IN COMMUNICATION

Effective communication of your mission involves a lot more than choosing the right words. The right words certainly help, but they are best served when used in conjunction with a well-established method.

As a leader, strive to incorporate the following six Cs of communication. Of course, there's always room for exceptions, but these six concepts will provide a firm foundation from which to speak, write, or otherwise communicate your message:

Clear. I believe in living life to its fullest, with no shades of gray. And that's how I communicate. I speak in black-and-white terms with punctuations from the rainbow, but with no gray areas! To avoid assumptions, your directives, directions, instructions, regulations, and interpretations should be stated as clearly as possible. Leave no stone unturned by asking the all-important question: "Do you have any questions?"

Concise. No one likes to listen to someone ramble on and on and on and on and on. You automatically shut the listeners off. Consequently, any important message you might have conveyed loses its impact amid the clatter and clutter. I have always instructed my staff to keep their memos limited to one page, their e-mails as concise as possible, and their sound bites positive and to the point. Don't digress from the subject matter and waste your listeners' time.

Here's an anonymous poetic nod to conciseness that you may remember and apply whenever the time comes:

> *Charm and wit and levity may help you at the start,*
> *But at the end, it's brevity that wins the public's heart.*

Consistent. Avoid the yo-yo effect of changing your message to meet the moods of the day. Nothing frustrates people more than a leader who gets swayed by the last person who whispered in his ear. Make up your mind, make a choice, and make the message consistent to all parties at all times. People like to follow a leader who walks the talk time after time. Of course, you're not always going to be right. But when you're wrong, you should want to hear about it so that you can do something about it. Without criticism, there is little chance for growth.

Credible. Make sure your message is real. People have a nose for bullshit, and once your words fail their sniff test, everything else you do or say goes in one ear and out the other. Consider the discount factor you apply to most things that are said to you; this will help you ensure that your word to others is true and credible.

You can count on hearing me scream, "That feces don't flush in Philly" whenever my sniff test registers positive to bogus claims or excuses.

You also need to be aware that whenever your message is a high-reaching one, lots of people will dismiss it as BS from the get-go. This may be a natural defense in today's cynical world, but there is a way to flank and overcome this defense mechanism of others: by resolutely delivering on all the Cs of communication. In time, doing so will establish your credibility in even the most cynical mind.

Courteous. "Hello," "Please," "Thank you," "May I," "Excuse me," and "I'm sorry" are all too often forgotten once we stop watching *Sesame Street*. But, in fact, these simple words and phrases are probably some of the most important and effective in the English language. Not to mention the simplest. It doesn't take much effort to be courteous and to demonstrate respect throughout the course of the day to everyone you encounter. It sets the right tone and gives your staff a standard to emulate. Since people react to good manners with complementary good thoughts and feelings, the greatest value of courtesy is that it naturally commands respect in return. And when people respect you, they are more willing to follow you. Plus, such politeness is not only good for business, but is a sign of a good person.

Current. Keep your people abreast of current developments in order for them to feel empowered and engaged. Speak in the present moment. Your team will appreciate your open line of communication. Old news is bad news because it signals to the individual that he or she is of minor importance in the pursuit of your dreams and goals. Avoid sending such signals by consistently sharing news and encouraging questions and curiosity from others. I'm a huge proponent of sharing e-mails from the public with my staff, immediately distributing information garnered from focus groups and other sources, and establishing a give-and-take between management and employees regarding everyone's current projects and results. Keeping people out of the loop has a tendency to make those inside the loop less effective.

THE MEAT OF THE MESSAGE

Imagine that you have just been put in charge of a business that is teetering on the brink of bankruptcy. . . .

Such was the position that David Stern inherited in 1984, when he became commissioner of the National Basketball Association.

Considering that for many years now the NBA has had a license to print money, you may find it difficult envisioning a time when the league was all but bust. But it was awfully close. When David took over, the NBA was awash in red ink. Seventeen teams—more than half the league—reported financial losses. Old fans were leaving in droves, and new ones were nowhere in sight. Management and players were at constant war. Drug use by players was rampant and painfully obvious. Sponsors were taking their advertising dollars elsewhere.

Into this maelstrom stepped "the Counterman."

David Stern had earned that appellation while growing up in the family business, a delicatessen in Manhattan. It opened early in the morning and didn't close until well after midnight. David mopped the floor, stocked the shelves, took orders, made sandwiches, made change, and, through it all, learned an unflagging work ethic. He also learned the priceless value of doing whatever it takes to make people satisfied. Soon, there was no aspect of the business with which he wasn't familiar. He was competent. He was confident. He was a communicator.

And when he arrived atop the NBA, he brought these skills with him and used them to virtually save basketball.

In a nutshell, David Stern created a clear and consistent mission for the NBA, and then set out to communicate it and instill it across the board. In short order, the NBA embraced David's vision to create a fan-friendly atmosphere, promote world-class athletics and competition, and establish a respectable arena in which all of this could occur. He has remained the unwavering voice of this multifaceted mission, and by all accounts it has been a tremendous success.

David credits his upbringing with providing the skills he used to successfully preach the mission of the "new NBA" to its misguided members and to the vanishing public.

"If you're a counterman, you have to learn how to take care of the customers," he said. "You learn their likes and their dislikes. You learn about them and their families. You learn to smile and to talk with them. You learn what keeps them coming back."

Under his leadership, the NBA not only avoided death, it came roaring back to life. It has become an international attraction, followed in scores of countries. It is an entertainment empire. Revenue has increased 500 percent since David took the helm. Eight franchises have been added. The catchy slogan "I love this game!" became one of the most memorable in the history of marketing.

For a long time, a story circulated about a now legendary meeting between Stern and some television network moguls. To make his point, the commissioner, who is five feet nine, suddenly leaped up from the plush carpet onto the polished mahogany conference table and began to stride up and down, gesturing theatrically to make his point.

Now that's using some serious body language!

The others gaped at the sight of this feisty little man with the razor wit walking back and forth across the tabletop; eventually they were won over.

True story?

"As a rule," David said slyly, "I don't stand on tables." He paused for effect. "But I confess that I am an inveterate pacer."

It's one of those stories that, if not true, ought to be. Whatever the point he was communicating, his listeners got it.

David Stern pulled the whole league back from the brink. In the process, his ability to articulate his vision, focus on his goals, and maintain an open line of communication within the entire NBA resulted in his being regarded as the best and most effective commissioner in professional sports.

And, as the story goes, he can still slap together a mean corned beef on rye.

LIGHTS, CAMERA, ACTION!

After quietly observing two fascinating friends of mine at separate locations—*on location* of their respective movie productions, that is—I asked them what they believed was the secret to their success in achieving their vision, especially when members of their team included megapriced, egotistical, highly talented superstars.

Barry Josephson—currently the head of Josephson Entertainment, formerly president of Worldwide Production for Columbia Pictures, and notably responsible for such blockbuster hits as *Men in Black, Air Force One, In the Line of Fire,* and *Bad Boys*—said that selection of the cast and crew is paramount, but that overall success is predicated on effectively communicating your vision.

He described his script as his first line of communication. This document details the game plan for the movie and provides his actors with a "forum" for them to voice their concerns and suggestions. Through an open and honest dialogue with the likes of Harrison Ford or Clint Eastwood or Will Smith or Tommy Lee Jones, Barry has maximized the opportunities to clarify his mission and engage their enthusiastic participation.

What do you think of the script?

What is your impression of your role?

What do you feel about . . . ?

I had the pleasure of making a cameo appearance in Barry's movie *Like Mike.* While on the set, I watched and admired how he talked *with* (and not *to*) his stars, Morris Chestnut and rapper Bow Wow. And I was impressed with his ability to motivate the handful of NBA all-star players who were also recruited to provide cameos in the movie.

Barry used clear, concise, and courteous instructions (not

demands). Questions were encouraged and noted, and solutions were readily available with an eye toward the movie's vision. He was passionate in his responses, and there was a feeling of concern and caring. His stars, not surprisingly, responded in kind.

Speaking of passion, that was one of the two qualities that writer-director-producer M. Night Shyamalan defined as necessary elements in the success of his movies. The other was conviction—another great C word!

Considering the tremendous success of Night's movies, such as *The Sixth Sense, Unbreakable,* and *Signs,* this passionate conviction is something that any leader would want to emulate.

The Sixth Sense was a sleeper, starting off slowly at the box office and then gradually scaring the wits out of millions of moviegoers worldwide to the tune of nearly $700 million. Topping that, in a sense, *Signs* set box-office records for Night and his star, Mel Gibson, capturing $60 million during its first weekend of release.

I love watching his movies and listening to him speak. That Shyamalan is one great storyteller!

Night has been compared to Steven Speilberg and Alfred Hitchcock in his ability to tell a tale. And since he writes all of his own material, he told me that he never feels insecure about accepting input from the likes of Mel Gibson or Bruce Willis or Samuel L. Jackson. He feels so confident in his thoroughly researched script, his ability to communicate his vision, and his handpicked actors' ability to live their roles and achieve their goals that, when questioned by his stars to explain his point of view during a particular scene, Night believes that simple clarity and conviction and the passion of his message help his actors fully comprehend his mind-set.

And he is so confident with his direction and the words of

his script that he's not opposed to asking: "Do you feel there's another way your character can better express his emotion in this scene?"

Quite the inspirational leader, Night feels a sweet sense of satisfaction when his actors can top the lines he's written, as well as what he's written between the lines.

THE 93 PERCENT RULE

Communication experts reveal that 7 percent of any interaction is verbal (the actual words that you say), and the other 93 percent is composed of your body language, voice, intonation, syntax, and facial expressions. David Stern, for one, capitalizes on the 93 Percent Rule!

It's just as important to be conscious of these nonverbal communication tools as it is to consider the words that you use. Not only do they allow you to express emotion visually, but they can also reveal your true feelings if you are not aware of them.

Being half Italian (the other half is Irish), I tend to use my hands and arms a lot when I speak. In fact, after my first appearance on the *NBA on NBC* studio show in the winter of 2001, the executive producer, David Neal, came down from the eye in the sky to give me—and my arms—a little direction. He remarked that he was pleased with the content and flow of the conversation between Ahmad Rashad, Jayson Williams, Mike Fratello, and me. But then he added: "Pat, could you be a little less animated?"

I heard his message loud and clear: *Sit on your hands or disappear!*

So the following Sunday—same time, same channel, same seat—I made a conscious effort to keep my hands touching the top of the dais during my portion of the discussion. No stray hands waving in the air, no patting my partners on the shoulder, no punctuation of thoughts with a slap of my hands or a punch in the air.

I was pretty proud of my effort.

Well, the show ended and in strolled David. He made his way between the producers and the camera and lighting crew up to the front of the studio dais. I was hoping (silently praying) for a compliment. But instead, David said, "Pat, forget what I told you last week. Do whatever feels natural. We missed your energy level."

Yessss!

Speaking of nonverbal communication, I'm reminded of a favorite adage: "Of all the things you wear, your expression is the most important."

People know when you speak from the heart by watching your eyes (and your hands in my case!). When you communicate, maintain eye contact and focus on the receiver of your message. People know when you mean what you say and they also know when you're not talking turkey.

> **PAT CROCE POINTER:**
>
> Of all the things you wear, your expression is the most important.

Speaking of turkey, here's a great story that I've told occasionally at staff meetings to emphasize the point:

A turkey was speaking with a big bull. The turkey said, "I would love to be able to get to the top of that tree, but I don't have the energy."

"Well, why don't you nibble on some of my droppings?" the bull asked. "They're packed full of nutrients."

The turkey followed the bull's advice and pecked at a lump of dung. Soon he found he had enough strength to fly up to the first branch of the tree.

The following day, after eating more dung, the turkey reached the second branch of the tree.

The next day, he continued to eat more and fly higher. Finally, the turkey was proudly perched at the top of the tree. Unfortunately, at the same time, a farmer spotted him from his front porch and shot him right out of the tree.

The moral of the story: Bullshit might get you to the top, but it won't keep you there.

One interesting component of the 93 Percent Rule that takes bullshit completely out of the equation is found in the skill sets of talented negotiators. In a word, I am referring to *silence*.

In negotiation, one rule of thumb is that whoever says the number first, loses. So, in effect, silence usually wins in a bargaining situation.

For example, in July 2001, one of our star players, Aaron McKee, was a free agent and was coming off a great year. The 76ers had advanced all the way to the NBA Finals, and Aaron had received the NBA's Sixth Man of the Year award—quite an accomplishment.

Aaron's agent, Leon Rose, was negotiating with our general manager, Billy King, regarding Aaron's contract.

Billy knew that Aaron wanted to remain in Philadelphia, which was also his birthplace and where he had attended Simon Gratz High School and then Temple University. He was a homeboy hero.

Advantage Billy.

But Billy also knew that at least two other teams were interested in Aaron following the team's supersuccessful season. Plus, Aaron was the best friend of the team's superstar, Allen Iverson, who wanted Aaron to stay at all costs.

Advantage Mr. Rose.

Unfortunately, most times in professional sports, money talks and a player walks.

If Billy had spoken up and offered the salary number first, he would have lost because (1) maybe he could have kept Aaron on the team for a lesser figure and (2) if the number had been lower than Aaron felt was his due, then Aaron might have felt disrespected and possibly insulted enough to accept one of the other teams' offers immediately.

Billy danced around the topic, stressing all the positives that would benefit Aaron should he stay with the Sixers. Eventually, Billy managed to draw a number out of Leon Rose. From that point, it was just a matter of time. . . .

Aaron signed a seven-year deal with the Philadelphia 76ers.

As the Swiss say: "Speech is silver; silence is golden."

Another effective component of the 93 Percent Rule is actually a common cliché, but one that has a lot of truth to it. That is: It's not *what* you say (or don't say), but *how* you say it.

If you have a pet dog, as I do, than you know exactly what I mean. My terrier, Shemp, knows what my wife, Diane, and I mean by the tone and manner in which we say it. For that matter, so did my kids when they were little. They didn't understand the words as much as they understood the passion and intonation behind the words. So I think it's safe to say that anyone (staff, customers, vendors) as bright as your pets or your kids listening to your message will be more fully engaged if you consider and contour the way you communicate your message.

Here is a good exercise that clearly demonstrates the fact that *how* you say something can dramatically alter the meaning of what you say. Read each sentence aloud, making sure to accentuate the one word in the sentences that appears in boldface italics.

I didn't say I feel great.

*I **didn't** say I feel great.*

*I didn't **say** I feel great.*

*I didn't say **I** feel great.*

*I didn't say I **feel** great.*

*I didn't say I feel **great.***

It's funny how the meaning of these identical sentences changes dramatically when you slightly alter the emphasis of your voice on just one word.

Bear in mind the powerful impact of the 93 Percent Rule every time you're communicating your vision or detailing a game plan or sharing a thought with a customer, a member of your team, a city, or even a nation. . . .

A CIGAR, A TOP HAT, AND A SILVER TONGUE

There was nothing at all about him on the outside to suggest greatness.

He had a pug face that was flat and mashed in, giving him the low-slung, jowly look of a British bulldog. His paunch was a living testimony to his voracious fondness for beef and bourbon. He was seldom without a cigar roughly the size of a baseball bat.

He walked, in later years, with a cane. His voice was deep but raspy and had the acoustic quality of gravel being swished around the bottom of a metal bucket. He favored top hats and vests. But he had the soul of a poet, the heart of a lion, and above all, the golden throat of an orator.

Winston Churchill is judged by most historians to have been the greatest statesman and most inspirational leader of the twentieth century. And what most distinguished him was his ability to speak, to communicate.

Words roared out of his mouth like fire, igniting those around him and driving them to uncommon valor. He thrust his entire being into his message, and by the power of his conviction and communication, he lit—and led—the way for his countrymen. In one of the most revealing examples of leadership in all of history, Churchill rallied England from the brink of destruction at the hands of Adolf Hitler's merciless siege during World War II, and carried them to victory.

And what exotic weaponry did he have to throw against the German Luftwaffe in its relentless blitz of London? Words! And a combustible delivery.

Churchill knew, as every leader should know, that words have powers that transcend any weapon. Words can sing and sting, hurt and heal, sanctify and curse. And they hold an enormous sway over the masses. Men have entered fierce battles without hesitation, knowing that death lay waiting, for the sake of a rousing address by a charismatic commander.

Early in the summer of 1940, German forces were bombing London without letup. The British Empire was in flames, thousands of its soldiers lay wounded or dead, its weaponry was destroyed and disabled, and the country's spirit was all but crushed. Yet, there stood Churchill, defiantly telling Hitler in that bulldog-and-gravel snarl: "You do your worst, and we shall do our best."

He turned to his people and delivered a series of speeches that united his nation, inspired it to hold fast, and enthralled the rest of the free world. He vowed that England would resist to the end, would fight from the rooftops and the hedgerows, and would never, ever, yield.

With grandly sweeping rhetoric he told the House of Commons: "Let us therefore brace ourselves to our duties, and so bear ourselves that, if the British Empire and its Common-wealth last for a thousand years, men will say, 'This was their finest hour.'"

There he was, balding and dumpy and frumpy, flashing what became his signature gesture: that two-fingered V-for-victory sign. And the people were willing to follow him to the ends of the earth—some, to the end of their days.

He led by being brutally forthright and honest. He never tried to con those he was asking to follow him. And he offered no bullshit. When it came time to tell his countrymen what awaited them, Churchill confessed: "I have nothing to offer but blood, toil, tears, and sweat. We have before us an ordeal of the most grievous kind. We have before us many, many long months of struggle and suffering."

But before utter discouragement could set in, he thundered: "You ask, 'What is our aim?' I can answer in one word: Victory. Victory at all costs, victory in spite of terror, victory, however long and hard the road may be."

And victory became theirs, but not before Churchill's prom-ise of struggle came to pass. England lost more than 350,000 of her sons and daughters, but none died in vain. Just imagine the alternative if they had not fought at all. . . . Churchill did, and with the power of words translated his vision of victory to the people.

Churchill was modest about his role as leader, saying, "It was the nation that had the lion's heart. I had the luck to be called upon to give the roar."

His roar still resounds.

As a leader, your greatest achievement will be to communi-cate your team's mission with such resonance that it rings true straight through to the final celebration.

FOUR

Walk the Talk

As a leader, one of your most vital jobs is to set the standards for those you intend to lead, whether you're the head of a household, the champion of a charity, the captain of a team or club, the owner of a small business, or the CEO of a large corporation.

And then comes the hard part. You yourself need to live up to those standards. Every day!

One of the most crucial promises a leader makes, whether she knows it or not, is that she'll consistently rise above the bar that she herself sets. In other words, a leader promises to "walk the talk."

If she does not walk the talk, she becomes a hypocrite, a liar, and a leader who does not deserve to be followed. It sounds harsh, but it's an undeniable fact.

A worthy leader should be prepared to walk a mile in the shoes of those who

> **PAT CROCE POINTER:**
>
> One of the most crucial promises a leader makes, whether she knows it or not, is that she'll consistently rise above the bar that she herself sets.

stand behind her. And sometimes she will actually have to do so. If she is not willing to do so, why should she expect others to?

Now, I am not suggesting that the CEO needs to take mop in hand to prove her commitment (although I wasn't averse to cleaning a whirlpool in one of my SPT centers or escorting a fan to his seat at a Sixers game now and again). We are talking here about the standards, strategies, policies, and philosophies that need to be defined at the outset of—and modified if necessary throughout the life of—any endeavor.

And the foundation upon which these things must stand is, quite simply, integrity.

ME, MYSELF, AND INTEGRITY

There are as many ways to lead as there are leaders. That's because leadership is based on personality as much as on anything else. One leader may be the strong, silent type while another can be a dynamo of energy. The earnest and matter-of-fact straight shooter can be as effective as the imaginative and over-the-top visionary.

Applying the rules and strategies and theories set forth in this book will help any type of leader lead effectively. But there is one thing that needs to be firmly in place regardless of a leader's personality traits.

And that is integrity.

It's important to define what integrity is, and I will lean on the words of Dwight D. Eisenhower to define the word more lucidly than I could.

Eisenhower said, "In order to be a leader a man must have followers. And to have followers, a man must have their confidence. Hence, the supreme quality for a leader is unquestionable integrity. Without it, no real success is possible, no matter whether it is on a section gang, a football field, in an army, or in an office.

"If a man's associates find him guilty of being phony, if they find that he lacks forthright integrity, he will fail. His teachings and actions must square with each other."

I have found these words to ring true time and again. An effective leader needs to demonstrate consistently the courage and fortitude to do what is right, even when it isn't the most popular choice. And the definition of "right" can never waver, no matter what the circumstances. As a leader's integrity is established, he gains the resolute trust of those around him. Conversely, without the trust of his team, a leader—and the goals for which he is the steward—will forever be vulnerable.

Because of this sacred value of trust, there is only one way to achieve it. Trust can't be acquired through some shady deal or manipulative trade-off. Trust can't be bought, borrowed, or bequeathed. Trust is never for sale. People grant trust based on merit and worthiness and virtues and action. Trust must be earned!

Trust can be earned by living a life infused with a strong sense of integrity. And integrity can be firmed up by fostering these four characteristics: congruity, responsibility, reliability, and honesty. By keeping these qualities close to heart and soul, you will be able to say, "Trust me," and mean it.

1. Congruity

Do you walk the talk? Do you practice what you preach?

No matter what the topic, make sure your feet are always pointed in the same direction as your tongue. Don't let the life you lead stray from the words you speak.

Because I continuously preach the importance of the Ten Commandments of Service, I must in fact practice them religiously. If I expect all of my staff members to adhere to Commandment #10: Do It Now!, what would they think of me if I consistently procrastinated and put issues off until later? And what would they think if I ignored Commandment #6: Be Prompt and Professional, by always arriving to meetings five or even fifteen minutes late?

Hypocrite! That's what they'd think of me. And they'd be right.

As I have stated, I believe that if you're late, you're rude. You're also inconsiderate, discourteous, thoughtless, unorganized, and lacking in discipline. My staff in every one of my business and community ventures has always known that to be my belief. Consequently, I never want to give them a chance to think of me in such derogatory terms. I cherish their respect and admiration and trust too much to place it in jeopardy.

Unfortunately, Commandment #6 became a national issue during the off-season prior to the Sixers' magical run in 2000–2001.

In the summer of 2000, our head coach, Larry Brown, publicly criticized the behavior of team superstar Allen Iverson. A.I., though incredibly talented, had begun to act extremely unprofessional. He was late for meetings and apathetic in practice, and often claimed lame excuses in order to skip both. As a result, Larry's frustration grew to the point that he continually informed the press of his desire to trade "the Answer."

In fact, a trade was planned where four teams would rearrange the employments and environments of twenty-two players. But for a few minor details, the triggers were about to be pulled. Uh-oh. I didn't want to see A.I. leave the Sixers.

I called Allen to inform him of the impending trade scenario and the coach's rationale. Allen was livid. He didn't want to leave Philadelphia. He was the main reason for the resurrection of the franchise. And he wanted to finish what he had started.

I told him that I couldn't side with him, even though I didn't want to see him wearing any other team jersey, because his actions were inexcusable and indefensible.

During a heated hour-long conversation, Allen said that he realized he had "f—d up." He promised that he would be on time for practices, he would work out with the weights, he would do all the little things the coach requested of him. And to top it off, he said that he wanted to be the team captain and to be a real leader on the team.

Yesssss! I thought.

I replied very calmly, "Bubba, that's music to my ears, but you've got to walk the talk. No one has more job security on this planet than you if you keep it real with your words."

The rest is history. To his credit, the following glorious season saw Allen Iverson earn the NBA's Most Valuable Player award as he led the Philadelphia 76ers to a fifty-six-win season and a trip all the way to the championship round for the first time since 1983.

2. Responsibility

Do you take responsibility for your actions and admit your mistakes?

I've learned through experience that you can delegate authority, but you can't delegate responsibility. The big R is yours to keep, whether you like it or not. You must assume responsibility for your followers' actions; otherwise, you violate the leadership contract, and trust is lost.

It is imperative to realize that being a leader is not at all about being the boss. It is all about assuming responsibility.

You will notice that when a worthy leader has to right a wrong, she will utilize the "3-R" approach of responsibility, regret, and remedy. The first step she will take is to assume **responsibility** for her actions and/or the actions of her people, and she will clearly state, "It's my fault." (Unfortunately, this was not the case in the corporate scandals that recently rocked the business world. Many CEOs who were basically caught red-handed refused to own up to their actions, thereby further angering disgruntled employees, stockholders, Wall Street, and Congress.)

Next, the embattled leader will demonstrate **regret** by apologizing to all of those offended, sincerely stating: "I'm sorry."

And finally, a leader will offer a **remedy** to fix the problem and alter the cockeyed course in the right direction, stating with clarity and conviction: "This is what we will do. . . ."

When I was first looking to hire a general manager for the Sixers in 1996, I asked around the league for recommendations. I was confident in my knowledge of finance, sales and marketing, public relations, community relations, and customer relations, but I was unfamiliar with the field of basketball relations.

In all, I interviewed six candidates. The biggest of those names were Chuck Daly and John Gabriel. John's contract as the general manager of the Orlando Magic was running out, and I began courting him. Unfortunately, but completely within the ethics of business, he used my offer as leverage and eventually renewed his contract with the Magic. Chuck, on the other hand, was having too much fun making too much money with too little stress as a television commentator. He said the timing wasn't right.

I hired the best of the rest in a man—Brad Greenberg—who had strong NBA recommendations but no experience at all in the general manager position. My mistake.

My new general manager, in turn, hired a rookie coach. Our mistake.

So an inexperienced owner allowed an inexperienced general manager to hire an inexperienced head coach. The result was predictable, at least with the benefit of hindsight, which, as we all know, is always a perfect twenty-twenty.

Mea culpa. Mea culpa. Mea *maxima* culpa!

But what's worse than making a mistake is not admitting it and correcting it. I would live with mine for that horrible losing year, and then I would rectify it.

It is a universal law that we all make mistakes. It is a normal process in all of our lives. What we do to make amends is what separates leaders from losers.

People will forgive a mistake due to poor judgment of the mind, undisciplined exuberance, or even a mental fart. But they will never forgive or forget the mistake one makes by covering up the first mistake. This grievous act reflects poor judgment of the heart and soul, and can leave you with a label that you won't soon be able to peel off.

On the day after my first season as president of the Sixers ended, I stood in front of a room filled with Philadelphia's top sports reporters and told them that I had made a mistake in my hiring of both coach and general manager. I was confessing my blunder in public. And I was apologizing. I said, "I'm sorry. I made a mistake."

I don't think I've ever done anything that was quite as demeaning or humiliating as standing in front of the media and taking all their shots. But I believe that, because I adhered to the 3-R approach, from that day forward I had earned and maintained the respect and trust of the press and the public.

As I wrote in my book *110%*, under Strategy #66: Own Up to

the Boo-Boo, "It's only those who never do anything who never make mistakes."

3. Reliability

Are you available in the moments that matter? Are you accessible in times of turmoil? Do you honor your promises and commitments?

One of the very first things I did when I took over as president of the 76ers was to get myself a godfather. I recruited the consultative services of the undisputed, uncontested, unquenchable Godfather of Basketball in Philadelphia.

William Randolph Hill. Known to all as Sonny.

Sonny was, and is, *da man*. He organized his first summer basketball league in 1960. He was still playing professionally then, a flashy five-foot-nine guard in the Eastern League who never met a shot he didn't like. When developing that first league, Sonny had to recruit some of his guys (among them Wilt Chamberlain) in order to give his fledgling organization instant cachet and credibility.

Today, the Charles Baker Memorial League is an institution. Pros come from all over the country to play there in the summer. It's a proving ground for them, much like the famous Philly "gym wars" are for boxers who come to the City of Brotherly Love to find out how tough they really are.

In addition to the Baker League, there is the Sonny Hill Community Involvement League, a youth-oriented league that annually consists of four dozen teams and has sent more than twenty-five thousand youngsters through its program since 1968. But—and this is the key part—it isn't just about basketball. The program offers tutoring opportunities and career counseling. The kids are tracked and monitored, starting as early as fifth grade and going through high school.

This is a glowing example of commitment—the fruits of a man who has thrown himself body and soul into his project. And you know what else? He is technically a volunteer . . . a very reliable volunteer. And so are all of those who help run the camps.

Sonny is equally flamboyant in dress and speech. But he doesn't just talk the talk; he definitely walks the walk. And he does so with a certain swagger.

He is the personification of walking the talk. His network of contacts is staggering. There isn't anything that goes on in the game of basketball, and certainly not in Philadelphia basketball, that he doesn't know about.

I relied heavily on Sonny for his basketball experience, his leadership skills, his vast network of relationships, and most important, his friendship. And I was never disappointed. His reliability frankly stunned me. Whenever I needed him, he was there. In some cases, he anticipated my need and just showed up.

During that somber press conference when I was telling the world that I had made a mistake and therefore had to dismiss the team's general manager and coach, who do you think was positioned behind me at the podium, literally watching my back?

Sonny.

Every game for five years, when I would walk the concourse greeting fans prior to tip-off, who do you think covered the same concourse, pressing flesh, backslapping, and generating miles of smiles with an attentive ear and his outrageous approach to life?

Sonny.

And when I continually preached my vision of a world-class organization that would service the basketball needs of the city regardless of race, color, or creed, who do you think helped open the doors to the African-American community?

Sonny.

4. Honesty

Do you tell the truth? Do you think the truth? Are you honest in word and deed?

A leader's honesty has to be a constant policy—at work or at play. Anything you do outside the office or away from your team may seem like an unrelated matter. But it's not. Your actions in all areas of your life can affect your position as a leader, and you must be aware of this fact.

Emerson said: "The ancestor to every action is a thought."

I saw a TV program where an industry expert evaluated CEO candidates for their honesty and character. You'd think that he would exclusively consider the candidates' work histories, emphasizing pacts made, deals struck, business relationships, and business tendencies.

But when he got right down to it, it was these prospective executives' actions outside the office that revealed the most about them: 33 percent of these candidates, it turns out, cheat at golf!

Makes you wonder . . . is dishonesty really worth it?

Your reputation is more important than a twenty-dollar Nassau. And your reputation is always on the line, whether you're on the job or off. Your actions in everyday life naturally influence your reactions in the business world. Even those actions that you think are going unseen.

Over the course of two months covering the 2002 NBA playoffs as a sports commentator for the *NBA on NBC*, my field producer, Pete Radovich, and I traveled countless miles to report on games in over a half-dozen cities. Between the wild crowds and bright lights and intense playoff action, we experienced a lot of downtime.

And without fail, whether we were in an airport or a restaurant or a hotel lobby, we would marvel at the courtesy—or lack thereof—of our fellow Americans.

Since Pete and I are such avid people watchers, we turned our observations into a game that we called "Good Samaritan of the Day."

It was not as easy as it sounds.

Most days, we'd spy people performing simple tasks like holding the door or assisting with the retrieval of luggage from the overhead compartment. Occasionally we'd see someone engaged in the unusual act of assisting a stranded motorist.

But mostly, we saw men and women whose only concern was protecting their own minuscule space on this third rock from the sun. They were not interested in anything other than getting where they were going. They would say or do anything, so you'd better get out of their way!

One off day, when there was not a Good Samaritan to be found, Pete told me an amazing story of someone who could have been a candidate for our "Good Samaritan of the Year." He was speaking of his wife, Nancy.

He described her as being as honest as the day is long.

It's funny how honesty and courtesy have a way of walking hand in hand.

One night, as she waited at JFK Airport in New York for Pete to arrive from a game in Portland, Oregon, she saw a group of men load their luggage into a van and then quickly pull away. In their wake, Nancy noticed they had left something stranded on the luggage cart. She got out of her car to investigate and realized it was a leather portfolio containing someone's personal life story: cellular phone, keys, credit cards, a diary, an airline ticket, and a passport.

This oversight was going to be that someone's personal nightmare.

When Pete arrived, Nancy showed him the portfolio and explained what she had seen. After further examination, Pete concluded that the portfolio's owner was a twenty-one-year-old Norwegian sailor who was returning home from working on a ship in the Caribbean. He had landed at JFK Airport and was transferring to Newark Airport in New Jersey for his flight to Norway.

Or at least that's what he thought.

Upon even closer inspection, Pete discovered a hidden compartment from which he removed seventy-one $100 bills—that's $7,100 in cash!

Finders keepers, right?

Pete admitted that, naturally, the thought of keeping the money crossed his mind. They could just return the portfolio's contents to the airline in the JFK terminal, which would then track down the sailor and help him get safely home.

As Pete fingered the cash, Nancy painted a picture of a twenty-one-year-old kid who had just lost his entire paycheck and all forms of identity and was stranded in a foreign country with nothing but a world of trouble.

Nancy inspired her husband—battle-weary from an extra-long travel day—to step on the gas and drive immediately to Newark Airport in hopes of finding the lost soul. Along the way they let their minds wander through the many ways they could spend their newfound treasure.

Fortunately, in this circumstance, vision without action is nothing but a daydream.

When they arrived at the Scandinavian Airlines counter at Newark Airport, Pete and Nancy noticed a young man, obviously a wreck, being consoled by his friends.

"Stefan?" Pete said. "I think you forgot something."

The sailor's eyes widened like saucers as Pete pulled out the portfolio. "How? Where? I don't understand. . . ."

After some small talk and an emotional good-bye, Pete and Nancy turned to go.

"Wait!" Stefan said, and thrust a wad of bills into Pete's reluctant hand. "I insist . . . and thanks again!"

It was $1,000!

Pete said that he and Nancy had the time of their lives the very next day, enjoying the fruits of their honesty.

What would *you* have done in this same situation?

What thought crossed your mind?

Be honest. . . .

"TRUST ME" OR "SCREW YOU"?

Does what you say and do encourage trust in you?

Amazingly, you can take the four words we just discussed—congruity, responsibility, reliability, and honesty—and sum them up in two simple words: *Trust me.*

Yes, two simple words. Yet it's one of the most intense, powerful, and meaningful—not to mention fully loaded—sentences you can utter. Or have uttered at you.

It's something a man says to a woman when he asks her to be his wife. It's also something that a used-car salesman says to try to seal the deal.

Ultimately, it's a promise—and one that should never be taken lightly. When one hears these two words, there needs to be a reason to accept the promise that accompanies them. And it is the speaker's responsibility to provide that reason.

That's why saying it is as risky as accepting it.

Will you be able to be a good husband for the next fifty years? Will that 1995 Chevrolet you personally guarantee still be running in fifty days?

As risky as it may be to say "Trust me," it is a risk that a leader must take, and a promise that a leader must make. That is, if he wants to be a *successful* leader.

Unsuccessful leaders don't even consider seeking the trust of those in their charge—they may even feel it is unnecessary or below them. For some of these individuals, as we have seen so frequently, "Trust me" really means "Screw you." And marginal leaders often just assume that they have their workers' trust, though they never take steps to earn it. Invariably, trust is not given to either of these types.

To be a successful leader, remember: trust has to be sought and it can't be bought. It has to be earned in everything you say and do . . . even if it means living up to a promise to do something on the fringe of sanity.

Throughout the Philadelphia 76ers' enchanted playoff run in the spring of 2001, a fellow lunatic from South Philly kept bugging me to stage another death-defying stunt to spur on the already fervent city. Angelo "Aces" Borgesi invited me to his workplace to discuss his idea. But he didn't work in an office; he was talking about a bridge. Specifically, the Walt Whitman Bridge, which spans the Delaware River and connects Pennsylvania and New Jersey.

It does so, I might add, in large fashion.

At its peak, the Walt Whitman Bridge is four hundred feet high. It is a serious span.

"We'll climb the girders," Aces cheerily told me, "and then we'll hang a humongous banner." Like seventy feet by six feet.

In a rare moment of sanity, I declined.

PAT CROCE POINTER:

As risky as it may be to say "Trust me," it is a risk that a leader must take, and a promise that a leader must make.

But my buddies Aces and Sonny Leuzzi, and their mountain-goat cronies, wouldn't let me off so easily. They pestered and persisted, cajoled and kidded. Finally, I gave in. "If we get to the NBA Finals," I promised, "I'll climb that bridge and hang a banner that can be seen from three states."

But, of course, I couldn't do it by myself. I had to trust the experts.

Aces and his crew know every inch of that bridge. They do the painting. They do the repairs. They are used to working up in that rare air. They could probably walk up and down among the cables and girders in their sleep. So while I had decided to place my absolute trust in them, that doesn't mean I wasn't nervous. Though I knew these capable men would pilot me through the mission, there still were butterflies the size of 757s flying around in my guts doing wild barrel rolls and loop-the-loops.

I knew these guys were brave, but I also knew they were not stupid. Ninety percent of their job is preparation, and they don't take the first step without ensuring that they've got the proper equipment and have planned the procedure to its smallest detail. One of these details was to make sure I did not accidentally become the Bird Man of the Bridge. So they hooked a safety belt on me, and placed a clip on each hip.

The climb up went smoothly and—thank you, Lord—without incident.

The cables upon which you walk are a good foot wide, so there is enough room to put one foot in front of the other instead of having to shimmy. A couple of the bridge crew preceded me to the top, to make sure, they said, that the hawks weren't in their nest.

"Excuse me," I said with the city of Philadelphia shrinking below us. "Would you repeat that, please?"

"Hawks. There's a hawk couple and they've made this bridge their home. They've built a nest."

"I'm sorry, but it must be the wind. I thought I heard you say *hawks.*"

"I did."

"Hawks? You mean, like, birds of prey?"

"That is correct."

"Hawks—with an *s*? *Two* of them?"

"At least."

"Hawks? Meat eaters?"

"Yes."

"The ones with talons? And sharp beaks?"

"That's them, yep."

"And they've built a nest up here?"

"Yes."

"And seeing as how this is their home, they would probably not welcome intruders, would they?"

"No, they would be quite upset," Aces replied. "In fact, they don't like to be disturbed at all."

"Well then, could you make sure they know we're not here to sell them aluminum siding? Could you tell them we're just passing through? And if there's a toll, we'll pay it, gladly, and they can keep the change?"

Luckily, the hawks were not at home. Shopping, maybe . . . for fresh meat. And their home looked like it could easily accommodate a six-foot-tall human with a goatee and glasses.

At the top of the bridge, we all did our part to drape the banner. It read: GO SIXERS, BEAT L.A.

Though our hopes were as high as the hawks' nest, the Lakers proved to be too good. The Sixers won the first game, but then lost the next four. L.A. won its second straight NBA championship. But the Sixers, with all their heart and hustle and grit and gristle, still left the city with a warm glow and a tale to tell for the ages.

When you establish a strong sense of integrity and gain the trust of others, your potential increases exponentially. When people know that you walk the talk (no matter how high up in the air), they are more apt to walk with you and listen to you. It is at this point that your leadership can work wonders, providing that you stay the course of your vision and keep adding to the kitty of actions, ideas, goals, and good deeds.

I am a strong proponent of listening to others in order to learn more about yourself and the world around you (see chapter 5, "Listen with a Leader's Eye"). It is through knowing and working with many great people who were filled with integrity and did good works that I came to truly understand the importance of this quality. I like to share these stories from time to time to better illustrate what it means to live with integrity as your North Star.

> **PAT CROCE POINTER:**
>
> When people know that you walk the talk, they are more apt to walk with you and listen to you.

Here are four stories of influence, inspiration, intensity, and insomnia: the wonderful side effects of a leader's life lived with integrity.

INFLUENCE OR INFLUENZA

Every day, you have the chance to do or say something that will cause ripples of influence that wash against lives. You have the influence that comes with being a friend, an enemy, a boss, an employee, a spouse, a parent, and the leader of strangers.

You may not be the leader of a country. Or the CEO of a Fortune 500 company. Or the coach of a professional sports franchise. Or even the highest-level manager at your own organization. But no matter who you are or what you do, you do have influence, and it's far beyond what you might imagine.

It has been estimated that in a typical day you will be influenced by at least four people, and you in turn will influence four others. And in your lifetime, at least ten thousand folks will be touched by your words and deeds and expressions.

Influenza isn't nearly as contagious or as easily spread as your influence!

You will exert this influence by your actions and reactions, by example and by sentiment. Some of that influence will be subtle. Some subliminal. Some overt.

There are certain professions in which influence is obvious and ongoing. The teacher. The doctor. The pastor, rabbi, priest, or preacher. As for the rest of us, someone, somewhere, is always watching. And listening. And deciding: *She's right about that.* Or: *Glad I heard that.* Or: *I might try that.* Or: *That's an interesting approach.* Or: *If he can do it, then so can I* (this thought has always been a great motivator for me).

Just as leadership need not be reserved for the select few, so it is with influence.

In fact, they are intertwined, influence and leadership. Because the way you lead, the way you get people to follow you, is to influence them to believe in you and/or your vision, and by giving them a sense of empowerment and self-importance.

Influence can be applied via a phone call, a memo, an e-mail, a pat on the back or a kick in the butt, or something so short as one word . . . *thanks.*

It need not even be spoken. It can be nothing more than a

glance. A stare. A glare. A smile. A wink. A thumbs-up. The finger. A two-finger victory pose. Sometimes, actions truly speak
louder than words.

At every turn, someone somewhere is trying to influence
somebody else: *Do this. Try that. Follow me. Forget him. I believe. I think. You can. They won't. Watch this.*

The more effective your leadership skills, and the more apparent your integrity, the greater your influence. The same
holds true for the people who influence you.

Such interaction and give-and-take is the stuff that makes
this world a better place. Consider the people who influence us
the most, individually: we never forget them! That's because
they have a special place in our heads and in our hearts. When
you have a minute, think about those people who displayed
such integrity and commitment that they actually changed your
life.

I started making my own little list of some special people
who've touched my life with an influence that spurred me to action.

The first name that came to mind was Julie. Julie was the
nurse who worked the graveyard shift at the Hospital of the University of Pennsylvania during my two-week stay there after I
nearly lost a leg in a motorcycle accident in the summer of
1999. She was there to attend to whatever I needed—to reposi-
tion my shattered leg, to replenish an IV, to empty a bedpan,
and to provide mental support as well.

Often she showed up before I could even call for her help. It
was as though, through an extraordinary commitment to her
job, she had developed some form of extrasensory perception
that allowed her to know in advance when she was needed.
What a wonderful gift. Her influence upon me went beyond
the obvious physical care. I promised myself that when I got out

of the hospital I was going to be more compassionate, more attentive, and more attuned as a person.

More like Julie.

I left the hospital with my leg intact, and with something just as important in addition—the influence of a person who helped me resolve to be a better person.

Another name that comes to mind is that of Sister James Regina. A nun with an agile mind and hands quicker than Muhammad Ali's in his prime.

I flash back to the eighth grade. I can still see her looming over me, patient beyond belief, pointing her ruler at the blackboard helping me diagram sentences and acquire grammatical precision, and then stilling my restless bones with another whack from that same trusty ruler.

She ministered to both brain and body. Most important, she instilled in me the desire to shoot for perfection, an understanding of the importance of attentiveness, and the desire to see a task through to completion. Her influence has stayed with me these past thirty-six years. And, God willing, will do so for thirty-six more.

The next name that flashed in my mind was the special friend who loaned me four thousand dollars when I had nothing but lint in my pants pockets. The money came without questions or strings attached.

I needed capital to bankroll my own physical therapy practice. Yet all I had was hope and optimism and a vision. In terms of tangible assets, that's not much to put up for collateral. But this friend didn't ask for collateral. He didn't, in fact, ask for anything at all.

Funny how fathers tend to be that way, isn't it?

So those were the first three names of influence that appeared before me like flashes of bright light.

Julie the nurse. Sister Regina the teacher. And the original Pat Croce.

They're leaders in my mind. Their influence has been immeasurable.

How about you; who's on your list? Can you name two teachers from whom you learned vital lessons? Can you name a friend who came rushing to your aid, no questions asked and no judgments made, when you were in desperate need? Can you recall a stranger who performed an act of mercy or kindness or compassion, and left without expecting anything in return from you?

These are the people who have influence. And every day, you have the opportunity to be among them. As a respected leader of your business or community or club or family, you have more than the opportunity; in fact, you have the responsibility. Use it wisely, because influence, like fame, can be fleeting.

> **PAT CROCE POINTER:**
>
> The servant-leader tempers passion with compassion, inspires through his actions, and is willing to listen to and learn from those he leads.

INSPIRATION IN A HABIT

To be a good leader, learn what it means to follow. To be an inspired leader, share of yourself. To be a great leader, develop the heart of the servant.

The servant-leader tempers passion with compassion, inspires through his actions, and is willing to listen to and learn from those he leads. He keeps his door and his ears open, and knows when to close his mouth.

The servant-leader has a strong sense of empathy. She knows that whatever needs to be done is not beneath her, and that there should be no limit to sharing ideas, gripes, compliments, solutions, and dreams. She understands that people don't really care how much you know until they know how much you care.

Ultimately, an effective leader is willing to take responsibility, give endless support, cover others' backs, and keep the team moving forward. No matter what it takes.

These concepts may be at odds with many people's impression of leadership. Misconceptions about a leader's role are as widespread as they are varied. Some people believe a leader has the right to make unquestioned demands. Others have come to think that a leader need not ever interact with those "below" him. For some, the idea that a leader should serve anyone at all is ludicrous.

That is why the nightly news is sprinkled with stories of corporate chieftains who think that doing well in business has nothing to do with doing good. They're a scary lot. Sure, you want to do well in your chosen field, but unless you do good, then doing well is not good enough.

As Voltaire said: "Every man is guilty of all the good he didn't do."

I believe the best way to feel great is to do good while you are working on doing well. It's easier to understand the principle of leading by serving—and on a deeper level, leading by inspiration—if you watch it in action. I've had the opportunity to be an active witness of a particularly inspiring woman for many years.

She is a retriever . . . of lost souls. She plucks them from the streets, the castoffs and the forsaken who have fallen through society's cracks.

She takes them in—the homeless and the aimless—and

gives them shelter and food and a small sense of comfort. This alone would be magnanimous work, but Sister Mary takes her job a step further. She strives to help these forlorn souls help themselves. Anyone can give a handout. Sister Mary gives something better: self-respect. She helps in a way that does not make them dependent upon that help, and she insists that they become self-sufficient.

In so doing, their dignity is restored to them, along with their self-esteem, their hope, and their dreams for a fulfilling future.

That is leadership at its shining best.

Sister Mary Scullion started a shelter and a recovery program in 1985 in the mean streets of North Philadelphia. It is called Woman of Hope, and it provides permanent residences for the homeless and mentally ill. It is a lifeline that has reeled in many lost souls and returned them to the fold of the community.

In 1989, Sister Mary created Project H.O.M.E., which started as an emergency winter shelter and has grown into a nationally recognized organization. Today, the project maintains more than $50 million of equity in housing and other economic developments, vital after-school programs, adult learning classes, and community gardens.

That's right, gardens! Splashes of greenery in bleak and blighted urban settings. A place for things to grow and bloom, and in so doing, reaffirm that life is good and can blossom with a little help.

The basic provisions of Project H.O.M.E. are education and health care. Its ultimate aim is to help its residents break the cycle of homelessness and poverty.

When I first met Sister Mary, she lived at Saint E's (Saint Elizabeth's), a former convent that was made into a recovery residence for homeless men. The structure has four floors, literally and figuratively. As the men progress through rehabilitation and education processes geared toward reentering society, they move up a floor at a time. By the time they reach the roof, they're knocking on heaven's door.

The residents on the first floor, however, have reached rock bottom. They have just escaped life on the very brink, huddled on sidewalk steam grates or curled into cardboard boxes under bridges or overpasses. These are society's outcasts, regarded by society as lepers and treated by many as such.

But I have found them to be good men who just happen to be living on the far side of hope and success.

Many of the residents eat at the Back Home Café. You can, too, and I heartily recommend it. The café is a Project H.O.M.E. business entity that is open to the public for breakfast and lunch. The food is tasty and nourishing, and if you drop in, you're apt to have Tom Smith—or someone remarkably like him—cooking your grub.

Tom is forty-eight, looks at least ten years older, and wears his past on his seamed and crinkled face like a map of the bumpy road he's traveled. A mixture of crack, alcohol, and no place to call home will etch the years into you, double time and overtime.

One day over lunch, Tom was bubbling with good news, the joy streaming out of him. He had just graduated to the fourth floor of Saint E's, which meant he had reached the top of his climb back, and was qualifying to be readmitted to society.

He had also just passed his driver's license test, which served as tangible evidence of his coming independence. His voice was thick with pride.

"I feel like I'm somebody now," he said.

That's the idea of Project H.O.M.E.

Sister Mary and her followers work miracles every day—little miracles that snowball into huge ones. I'm proud to count myself as one of her flock. She is an inspiration to me. She is wiry and fiery. She runs marathons. She can cow the most powerful politician, and she can con the slickest cons on the corner. If she didn't invent the practice of "tough love," she sure perfected it.

She had a vision of educating and employing and empowering those whom society had given up on. She has far exceeded that goal. The grand result is that more than five thousand men and women have been helped by Project H.O.M.E., and the rate of homelessness on the streets of Philadelphia has been cut in half in the years since the project began.

As Sister Mary leads the unfortunate out of degradation and misery, she leads society out of ignorance and arrogance and misconceptions.

It is no wonder she was the recent recipient of the Leadership for a Changing World award, which recognizes the achievements of outstanding leaders who use their unique power to influence minds and inspire souls, with just the right splash of intensity.

INTENSITY SETS THE VISION ON FIRE

When it comes to walking the talk, I usually have a lot of walking to do. That's because I'm not afraid to talk, and to encourage others to do whatever it takes to get the job done. It's something that I preach all the time. Still, I've got to be willing to match the intensity I require from others. Fortunately, I'm more inclined to top that intensity level.

Every leader must be willing to match the intensity level that they require of others. This is at the foundation of walking the talk. If a leader can't meet the standard, then he or she needs to rethink those standards.

When I was a kid, I loved playing with a magnifying glass. It was always one of my favorite surprises at the bottom of a Cracker Jack box. I'd take the cheap little lens outside into the hot summer sun and try to create fire.

Not a big fire. Not a blazing fire. I just had the desire to create a little burn hole of fire.

If I held the magnifying glass steadily over a piece of paper, the intense sun rays would become focused through it like a laser beam and burn a hole right through the paper. It was amazing. I controlled the power of the sun!

But if my mind strayed or my hand wavered, if the focus of the sunlight's intensity faltered the slightest bit, then my mission would fizzle.

To this day, I use that magnifying glass as a metaphor for setting goals and achieving dreams:

Stay focused!

Whenever I set out on a new mission, I carry a mental magnifying glass and keep it firmly and steadily above the goal. All my resources are pointed through the lens in the same direction and for the same purpose and at the same intensity. When everything is in sync, it's like rays of sun converging on an unfortunate piece of paper . . . fire!

Individual strengths combine to form an even greater whole.

Think of how a professional pitcher focuses on that catcher's mitt. He stares it down, rears up, cocks his arm, kicks his leg, twists his hip, and whips his hand down, finally snapping his wrist and zipping a ninety-mile-per-hour fastball right into the sweet spot. All those intense physical motions are working separately, yet together, and are under the complete control of the pitcher's focus. (That is, if he's having a good day.)

Whether it's the way you prepare, your time management, your attitude, what you learn from others, or how you choose to reach your goals, it's the *intensity* of your focus that matters most.

As the saying goes: "Keep your eyes on the prize." Everything else follows with dead certainty. In my case, at full speed ahead!

Bill Gates, the founder of Microsoft, summed it up best when he said, "You know, the notion that a kid who thought software was cool can end up creating a company with all these smart people whose software gets out to hundreds of millions of people, well, that's an amazing thing. I've had one of the luckiest situations ever. But I've also learned that only through *focus* can you do world-class things, no matter how capable you are."

Like the leader of the PC revolution, this "P.C." also believes that you

> **PAT CROCE POINTER:**
>
> Whether it's the way you prepare, your time management, your attitude, what you learn from others, or how you choose to reach your goals, it's the *intensity* of your focus that matters most.
>
>

must maintain the focus of a brain surgeon when attacking goals and achieving dreams. And if you want others to display that intensity of purpose, then first you'd better do so—walk the talk—yourself.

Harold Katz will tell you if I've got what it takes. . . .

In October of 1995, I had lunch with Harold. It was just one in a series of lunches I had had with successful businessmen during a time in my life when I was looking for the next big venture. I was in the Vision Quest process.

I thought a nice conversation with Harold Katz—then the

owner of the Philadelphia 76ers—could result in some ideas and direction and possibly flip the switch on my cerebral lightbulb.

And boy oh boy, did it! I left that restaurant believing that one day soon I would actually own the Sixers. Harold spent the entire lunch venting about all the things that had been going wrong for him and his now lousy team. I listened as his frustration mounted, and my mind kicked into high gear. Suddenly, surprising even myself, I suggested that I buy 10 percent of the team and become the front man for him, relieving him of all the *agita*. Of course, he laughed. But he didn't say no.

Despite his laughter, the odds were proving better than if I had never asked in the first place. My dad always said if you don't ask, then the answer is always no. He had to be looking down from cloud nine, smiling.

So I began to apply a full-court press. And it all started with a simple phone call to Harold the day after our lunch. During the call I suggested that, since he didn't want to own the team with me, I should buy the entire team from him. He laughed again. But again, the answer was not no. It would not be my last phone call to Howard. Nor would that lunch be our last meeting. Far from it!

My persistence intensified, my focus magnified, and suddenly we were in the middle of a deal that included Comcast Corporation, a handful of the most powerful businessmen in Philadelphia, old and new sports arenas, another professional sports franchise (the National Hockey League's Philadelphia Flyers), and a whole lot of lawyers and money managers.

By March of 1996, we were putting the finishing touches on the largest sports deal in Philadelphia history. Finally, the big day came when the official announcement was to be made.

We went to the press conference at the Spectrum. Some of

the key players on our side of the deal spoke. Then I introduced Harold, and I kissed him.

He was asked by one of the media what had made him sell the team. He looked down the dais, pointed to me, and said, "Pat Croce called me fifty times!"

I laughed aloud with the audience, but inside I breathed a huge sigh of relief.

I can't tell you how many people told me afterward that if they'd known Harold was ready to sell, they'd have bought the team from him. How come I had been the lucky one?

Two words: intense persistence.

That memorable press conference is proof positive that your IQ is not nearly as important as your "I will." Because while there is a limit to the knowledge you can accumulate, there is no limit to your dreams and determination. As intensity is a value that I vigorously promote, it was rewarding to be able to embody this value as an example to those whom I would lead.

Whatever level of intensity you require of your team as a leader, you must at least match it in order to walk the talk.

INSOMNIA IS NOT IN MY DREAMS

When you place yourself out front in a leadership position, you invariably experience mental and physical highs and lows, triumphs and tragedies, that relate to your vision and all its attendant choices and decisions. In other words, you're going to face pressure, often of the full-court variety.

And sometimes, this pressure can keep you awake at night. Accepting ultimate responsibility for all matters in pursuit of turning vision into reality is a full-time job. Leaders need to know this, and to be prepared for sleepless nights and anxious hours.

Of course, the kind of leader who doesn't walk the talk probably does not lose sleep for concern about the product, the fans, the staff, and most other issues that a leader with integrity cares about. Unworthy leaders often don't even remember what they've said, instead walking in any direction that's convenient for them at any given moment.

There are times when, unbeknownst to others on your team, the view from the front is not all that appealing. Sometimes the lightning and thunder in the skies above are meant for your eyes and ears only. Yet you maintain constant hope that the goals you set and the action steps you list will help you maneuver through the Vision Breakdown toward the realization of the dream.

These are undoubtedly tense times. And yet, at day's end when your head hits the pillow and your eyes close, it is crucial that your mind finds a peaceful state for sleep. Whether you made progress, broke even, or even stumbled that day, you will grant yourself the ability to achieve sweet sleep so long as you've navigated the day's perils with energy, enthusiasm, commitment, and a strong sense of integrity.

Even still, you must remember that *should* happens. As in: you *should* have done this, or you *shouldn't* have done that. And *should* seems to stink even worse as it gets mentally regurgitated in the quiet of night.

In the business of professional sports, the media and the fan base are available for comment 24/7. And they're not shy. One word or action by you, even when you thought it was the right choice, can result in a painful day. And night!

I have discovered that, when lying in bed at night, the de-

gree of difficulty you face in trying to block out a negative
image or situation is relative to the potential damage that your
mind can create for it. In other words, the larger the perceived
trouble, the greater the angst.

What, me worry?

Yes, even I, the Prince of Positive Attitude and the Count of Carpe Diem, worry.

I know that worry is nothing more than an exaggeration of the imagination. I know that worry can cast a big, bad shadow from the tiniest of issues. And I know that action is the best antidote to worry. Yet that shadow sure looks pretty scary in the middle of the night, especially when it is accompanied by the sound of your churning stomach.

I faced the scariest such shadows the night immediately following the press conference at which I announced the

> **PAT CROCE POINTER:**
>
> Worry is nothing more than an exaggeration of the imagination. Worry can cast a big, bad shadow from the tiniest of issues. And action is the best antidote to worry.

firing of the Sixers' general manager and coach. It was one day
after the last game of my rookie season as president of the Sixers. I had eaten crow, faced the music, and now my stomach
was churning as the shadows swirled through the dark bedroom.
If I could only fall asleep; but no, my mind was racing. . . .

There was a sense of urgency and extreme stress that resulted from that losing season. We had won only twenty-two
games out of an eighty-two-game schedule. It happened to represent a 20 percent increase over the preceding year, but that
wasn't good enough. The fans, my customers, wanted a winning
season. And they wanted it Now!

My mind wandered trying to conjure up candidates for both

crucial positions. And my imagination released a stream of thoughts detailing the scary scenarios if my search and eventual hires didn't result in a qualified, guaranteed success.

My bedroom reeked with the smell of fear. My own fear!

Philadelphia sports fans are a passionate breed. They know their sports. They live and die with their teams. And they want to win at all costs. I could just imagine their acts of displeasure (verbal as well as physical) if my rose-colored glasses led to my new hires smelling anything short of a rose. The fertilizer would be tossed in my direction . . . at full force.

Here I was with just one year under my belt as team president, and now, by default, I'm also the team's general manager and head coach. Uh-oh. I could barely shoot a basketball, let alone coach a basketball team or select the talent required to field a winning squad.

Millions of Sixers fans (real and potential) and all of my business partners were depending on my making the right moves. The heat was on, and I could feel the pressure . . . especially when I closed my eyes that particular night.

It's funny how your imagination can be a double-edged sword—enabling you to dream glorious possibilities while also maintaining the ability to drive you deep into the depths of despair.

Since sleep was not an option that April night, and since my normal remedy of enjoying a book could not distract me from my concerns, worry became the option of choice. So I fed the monster. I got out of bed, walked downstairs to my home office, turned on the desk lamp, picked up a pen, and started sketching solutions to my problem.

Normally, the solution to this sort of franchise problem would involve hiring a general manager, who in turn would hire the head coach.

We had already tried that route. It hadn't worked.

So I let my overactive, sleepless mind go into overdrive and dream of a best-case scenario. Almost unconsciously, I wrote: "Hire the best damn coach available and then fill in the blank for general manager at a later date."

Eureka!

Essentially, I followed an exercise like that found in a Vision Quest—asking myself questions to stimulate thoughts and ideas, wishes and wants, possibilities and dream scenarios.

Why do it this way?

Who would I want if I knew I couldn't fail?

What if . . . ?

I knew I wanted someone with winning experience, someone with a marquee name and a calling card for the franchise. My pen wrote four names: Rick Pitino (head coach at the University of Kentucky), Phil Jackson (head coach of the world champion Chicago Bulls, whose contract was about to expire), Roy Williams (head coach at the University of Kansas), and John Thompson (head coach at Georgetown University). (I didn't know at the time that Larry Brown was planning to leave the Indiana Pacers at season's end.)

Before I turned off the desk lamp, I prepared a to-do list along with a list of people I planned to contact to help me evaluate my solutions.

Suddenly, the problem was illuminated. The possible solutions to the problem were noted. I did my best, and went to bed believing that God would help me do the rest. Ahhh, good night.

FIVE

Listen with a Leader's Eye

One hallmark of a great leader is excellent communication skills. This much is obvious. But what exactly makes a great communicator?

Is it a booming voice? A copious vocabulary? Across-the-board eye contact? Excellent storytelling chops? A knack for just the right touch of humor? An enthusiastic tone? An ability to synchronize body language with diction?

Of course, all these skills of communicating are valuable and should be honed. But none of them are even in the same ballpark as the single most important part of communication in a leadership situation:

Listening!

That's right! A leader must listen closely to the world around him or her to be able to react to it. He must listen to his team members in order to learn what they need to succeed. She needs to listen to her confidants in order to gather valuable information that aids in decision making. He must listen to his customers to ensure that his staff is fulfilling the supply side of the demand. She should listen to her competitors to accumulate the knowledge necessary to win the battle of business. And he should listen to his vendors to ascertain opportunities and possibilities for increased efficiency and growth.

Good listening skills educate, motivate, help innovate, build business, nurture trust, create a sense of inclusion, and are an invaluable resource. Bad listening skills, on the other hand, can lead to a world of pain.

The best listeners are those who learn to listen with a leader's eye. This supernatural-sounding skill doesn't call for magic spells, but when it's practiced and consistently applied, it does lead to magical results.

To listen with a leader's eye, keep the big picture in mind. Listen with an eye toward making unexpected connections. View the possibilities. See what the sources are thinking while they are talking. Observe the body language behind the words and identify the emotions. And keep the endless lines of communication that are coming in open to all things—the good, the bad, and even the ugly. Don't stretch a filter over your eardrums!

PAT CROCE POINTER:

Good listening skills educate, motivate, help innovate, build business, nurture trust, create a sense of inclusion, and are an invaluable resource. Bad listening skills, on the other hand, can lead to a world of pain.

LISTENING BETWEEN THE LINES

At the beginning of my first year as president of the Philadelphia 76ers, in the fall of 1996, I promised season-ticket holders that I'd have a meeting with them about halfway through the season. Prior to joining the Sixers, I had become ingrained with the "customer first" philosophy, and I was determined to bring that quality with me. Not nearly enough professional sports franchises seek out the fans for input. Mostly, they want the money and the loyalty, preferably unquestioned. I wanted us to be different.

I planned to thank the fans for their patronage, update them on some improvements and promotions that were in the works, and then listen to their concerns, questions, and suggestions. Sure, the team was awful that year, but even though I anticipated some frustration and unhappiness, I thought the fans would appreciate the franchise's new direction and be grateful for the opportunity to meet and vent. I even entertained the notion that they might just take it easy on me. Little did I know, I was headed for a public hanging.

My own!

The gathering was set for ninety minutes before the tip-off of a home game against the Los Angeles Clippers. And the timing couldn't have been worse. It was catastrophic! We had won only a dozen games while losing three dozen plus three. That's an ugly record of 12–39! The team was in utter disarray. The coach had resorted to publicly criticizing the players, and the players had lost a sense of commitment to the coach and each other. Even though there were more than thirty games yet to play, everyone knew the season was already a bust. And now, I was going out there to face our fans, the season-ticket holders, my customers. What was I thinking?

To make matters worse, the exact day and time of the season-ticket-holder meeting was the exact day and time of the NBA trading deadline, and we had no big trade to announce—to the fans' great, vocal displeasure.

Let's just say I felt like the pig that's headed for the roasting spit at one of those Hawaiian luaus.

And I was right; the fans roasted me. From my hiring of the wrong general manager and coach to my failure to fire up (or fire) certain unpopular players, the fans left no stone unturned. Or unthrown. They really let me have it.

I didn't want to hear what I heard, but I listened anyway. I didn't filter out any information. I came to the meeting without any prejudice, ignorance, or arrogance toward those who would be speaking. It's part of a leader's responsibility. If you really want to win, in any situation and not just in the field of sports, you have to hear out the concerns of all involved. And then you need to learn from what you hear, admit your mistakes, and work to improve. You have to own up to your actions as well as the actions (and inactions) of your staff. Once again, I repeat that, as the leader, you can delegate authority but not ultimate accountability or responsibility.

Anyone who would follow a leader understands that there must be an unwritten contract, a covenant of trust, which the leader upholds when the firing starts.

On that particular night, I would have preferred a bullet-proof vest and a crash helmet to a microphone when I approached the gathering. The fans-in-the-stands focus group turned into an unruly gang of vocal hooligans. But while much of what I heard was intense venting, there were also some truly worthwhile suggestions regarding ways the organization could improve. I don't mean just the Xs and Os and the personnel, although the fans' fury over the team's on-court woes was certainly the strong focal point. But in terms of presentation, arena ambience, and fan care, the people had some workable ideas and suggestions. And I heard what they said.

As a matter of fact, the very next day we began to set goals that would address some specific issues that arose that night. In a couple of months' time, some of those problems would be turned into positives. In a couple years, the franchise would become a model of fan relations and customer satisfaction.

But first, I had to listen. Intensely. Honestly. Attentively. With both ears and a leader's eye toward the future of the franchise and the benefit of our fans.

I can never overstate the importance of listening as a key component in the act of leadership. Likewise, I can never overstate the significance of *how* you listen.

If you're shuffling papers on your desk and looking away as an employee asks a routine yet important question . . . you're not listening.

If you cradle the phone between your shoulder and ear in order to rinse off the dishes as your mom or a friend tells you a story . . . you're not listening.

If you stare blankly into someone's face as he's speaking because your mind is busy thinking up your next wonderful response . . . you're not listening.

If you have that glazed-eye look that says, "My ears hear you but the rest of me is somewhere else" . . . you're not listening.

And in each of these cases, you're not alone. We've all been guilty of these poor listening practices. And we've all also been victims of such poor reception, so we should know how bad it looks, not to mention how bad it feels.

Effective listening involves more than your ears. It involves your eyes, for making contact and seeking insight. It involves your brain, for processing what is said and considering its full meaning. And it involves your attention span and complete focus, to keep your eyes and your brain and your ears on the job.

I like to call this kind of listening "listening between the lines."

Just as the expression "reading between the lines" suggests that you see more than meets the eye, listening between the lines allows you to maximize the information you get from a conversation. Not only does this give you an advantage, but your obvious interest in the speaker also gives her the sense that you value her thoughts and words.

In my experience, the best way to influence people to do what you want done is to find out what *they* want to do. And clearly, the best, most direct way to achieve this is to ask them. And then listen to what they say! And observe *how* they say it. And be keenly aware of not only what they are saying, but also what they are *not* saying. Frequently, what they're guarding against saying is more important than what they're giving voice to. It's up to you to listen between the lines to make such discoveries.

> **PAT CROCE POINTER:**
>
> The best way to influence people to do what you want done is to find out what *they* want to do. And clearly, the best, most direct way to achieve this is to ask them.

KEEP YOUR ATTENTION ON YOUR INTENTION

Of all the things that you may become in your life, becoming a good listener is among the most important.

You will be granted the gift of gaining knowledge, you'll be more in tune with the knocks of opportunity, and you'll strengthen the bonds in every relationship on your journey of life. Of course, you'll first have to see the value in listening. Then you'll have to find the desire to do so. Finally, and unfortunately, you'll have to work at it. And we're talking intense persistence.

The process itself is simple and consists of only two rules, which you can learn in less than a minute. Mastering the process, on the other hand, takes a lifetime. But it is time well spent.

1. Pay attention. Let the speaker know you're sincerely interested. Make eye contact and maintain it; don't gaze off into the distance or down at the ground. In your peripheral vision, make a note of the person's body language. (In fact, you can mirror his body language.) But focus primarily on the speaker's words and intent. Don't get caught yawning, sighing, daydreaming, or checking your watch. Don't step on the speaker's words with your own words or gestures, but feel free to offer an occasional head nod, an affirming "I see" or an engaging "I hear you" or a heartening "Interesting . . ." to maintain your listener's edge.

A great technique to enhance the conversation and further engage the speaker—client, customer, fan, employee, or family member—is to practice "active listening." This is where you paraphrase the speaker's words to ensure that you both fully understand the intent of the dialogue. For example, you could say, "So what you are saying is . . ." or "Let me get this right; you feel . . ." Use whatever tag expression works best for you, but be sure to encourage, not discourage.

2. Ask questions. First, asking questions lets the speaker know that you really are interested and have been paying attention. Second, it is flattering, and the speaker will become so emboldened that she won't hold back the good stuff once she sees that your interest is genuine. Third, it allows you to gently lead the conversation in a new and interesting direction. And fourth, asking questions gives you the opportunity to become more knowledgeable about the particular subject at hand. And it's a good idea, whenever you're stuck for a question, to pull out the most effective one of all, that old reliable standby: "Well, what do *you* think?"

You will do well to remember that you're not always going to like what you hear—or how it is stated—especially if you have specifically invited the opinions of others. But part of being a good listener is listening as attentively to the gripes and complaints as you do to the compliments.

Sam Walton said: "There are some rules that worked for me. But I always prided myself on breaking everybody else's rules, and I always favored the mavericks who challenged my rules. . . . In the end I listened to them a lot more closely than I did the pack who always agreed with everything I said."

When your audience, customers, fans, and staff are throwing them at you, the bricks hurt a lot more than the bouquets. But you can use those bricks to build something solid. The flowers, though nice and gratifying, will wilt and shrivel soon enough.

During the second year of my tenure as president of the 76ers, we created a marketing promotion offering a family "four-pack"—four tickets, four hot dogs, four soft drinks, and four newspapers—on Fridays. The price: seventy-six dollars.

It was a nice bargain, and it became an even better bargain when the team got good, and then an even bigger bargain when the team got really good. At last it became a fan favorite, and was always sure to please. Until March 2, 2001.

It was a Friday night, and the 76ers were hosting the Washington Wizards. An irate fan who had telephoned to ask some rather pointed questions was transferred to Joe Masters, our director of fan relations and one of my best buddies. Joe was our one-man complaints department, and this fan immediately tore into him.

How dare the Sixers so blatantly disrespect his family? How dare the Sixers commit such heresy and blasphemy? How dare the Sixers place the souls of the man and his family in such grave peril?

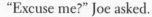

PAT CROCE
POINTER:

A leader's job is to
find a solution, not
find fault. To listen,
not to judge. To find
a silver lining within
every gray cloud of
a complaint.

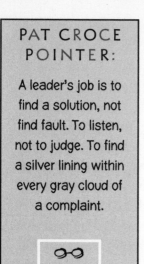

"Excuse me?" Joe asked.

"How," the man shouted, "do you expect my family to eat hot dogs on a Friday during Lent?"

Joe understood that a leader's job is to find a solution, not find fault. To listen, not to judge. To find a silver lining within every gray cloud of a complaint.

So he didn't suggest what the man might do with his hot dogs.

For example, give them to someone hungry. Or to an overzealous kid on the concourse. Or ask for a refund. (Or shove them in his ear!)

Joe listened to the man's complaint patiently, and then made it clear that he respected the man's position. He informed the man that he would seek a solution, and assured him that he would call him back promptly. I'm reasonably sure that as they hung up, the man was thinking to himself: *Right, he'll get back to me. Sure he will. When pigs fly.*

Well, that afternoon, if you'd looked up in the sky, you'd have seen bacon on the wing.

Joe talked with the arena's concessionaire, Aramark, and together they worked out an alternative. Joe called the man back and presented him with an option: You can substitute pizza for hot dogs.

Crisis averted. And a fan and his family won over. All because a good listener listened with a leader's eye and truly cared about the outcome.

PRESENCE WITH PRESENTS

The difference between good listeners and bad can be boiled down to one word: presence. A good listener is fully present. He's with you the whole time, hanging on your words, responding with insightful thoughts and probing questions, and maintaining consistent eye contact. A bad listener, on the other hand, might as well be drifting in outer space.

There's a strategy that I use to help sharpen my listening skills, especially the all-important aspects of focus and attention span. You can use it, too. It's a sort of mnemonic device that's simple, fun, and interesting. Most important, it works.

I call this exercise "Presence with Presents." The idea is that in conversation, you can enhance your presence by focusing on the "presents" that the other has to offer.

It's easy. Just pick out five characteristics about the person with whom you're talking, memorize these five "gifts," and then later, see if you can summon them from memory. Try asking questions like:

- How tall was he?
- What color were her eyes?
- Was there anything unusual about his speech patterns?
- How was her energy level?
- What do I remember most about so-and-so?

I consciously try to "be fully present" with everyone I talk to. In fact, it was my New Year's resolution last year. My wife, Diane, has been telling me that I have to learn to chitchat. I am naturally a world-class chatterer, but I have to constantly focus on conquering the "chit" portion of conversation.

It's difficult to be fully present. It can be enervating. And I have failed at this enterprise at times like everyone else. It is so much easier to offer a cursory nod and appear to listen while the mind drifts off, or to move through a conversation as if it were a fast-food drive-through.

But the effort you make to become a good listener will pay off. Help yourself by using the person's first name, observing and noting the color of her eyes, reading her body language, attentively grasping her words and considering their meanings, hearing what was *not* said, and then asking questions to further clarify her remarks.

Speaking of using a person's first name, it astonishes me how many people are admittedly "so bad with names." Most people say that they forget a person's name moments after they first hear it. Then what? Then you're stuck in an uncomfortable situation.

Even though I am known for and dedicated to remembering and using people's first names—no matter what!—I must admit that I have to work at it. You should, too. Remembering people's names when you first meet them, regardless of what you may believe, is a skill that can be mastered. It's an excellent quality to possess, not to mention an invaluable tool.

Why should anyone listen to you, as his leader, if you do not have the courtesy even to remember his name? Or why should someone purchase your product or service if you do not consider it important to call him by name? The answer is simple: he shouldn't.

Don't let it get to that point. And don't miss the opportunity to remember a person's name forever the instant you meet him.

Here's the method I use that can help you remember the name of every new person you meet:

Upon being introduced, make friendly and focused eye contact with the person. Keep good posture and positive body language, and approach him as the introduction is being made. Stick that first impression right in his face!

When his name is spoken (by himself or a third party), clearly and cheerfully repeat it out loud. Just go for it! Shake his hand, or share a hug if it is appropriate, and maintain eye contact as you repeat his name quietly in your mind.

As you're repeating his name, spell it out in your mind's eye. And as you're spelling his name, picture it being written out on a blackboard. Say his name to yourself one more time to complete the mental spelling bee.

During your conversation, casually use the person's name while making a point or asking a question. And finally, be sure to wish him a personal good-bye. I know the Name Game sounds like a lot of effort to remember just one little name, but what is the alternative? "Excuse me, I forgot your name?"

HERE'S A CRIB SHEET TO HELP YOU MASTER THE NAME GAME:

Say the person's name out loud. Say his name in your mind. Spell his name in your mind. See his name spelled. Say his name to yourself once more. Use his name in conversation. Wish him a personal good-bye.

Remember, there's no sound sweeter than the sound of one's own name!

THE LADDER OF FLATTERY

Dr. Joyce Brothers said, "Listening, not imitation, may be the sincerest form of flattery."

> **PAT CROCE POINTER:**
>
> By listening and responding positively to the thoughts and plans and schemes and dreams of others, at the most basic level you are giving them validation and empowerment.
>
>

They say that flattery will get you everywhere. I don't know if that saying is true, but I do know that listening will get you closer to everywhere than not listening. By listening and responding positively to the thoughts and plans and schemes and dreams of others, at the most basic level you are giving them validation and empowerment. And when each member of your team is empowered, your ability to lead grows exponentially.

We all need to practice listening. Constantly! Because in my experience and most likely in yours, too, most of us are not great listeners. We space out, we butt in, we do everything but pay full attention. Yet full attention is what's needed, both for your sake and for the sake of the person you're speaking with.

A great mnemonic device to improve your listening is called the "Ladder." It's a six-step process that is used by professional speakers and leaders alike, and it is quite effective in making great listeners.

Shaped like a six-rung ladder, the Ladder process looks like this:

L—*Look directly at the person speaking to you.*
A—*Ask questions periodically during the conversation.*
D—*Don't interrupt the speaker's train of thought.*
D—*Don't change the subject.*
E—*Empathize with the feelings of the speaker.*
R—*Respond, both verbally and nonverbally. (In my case, nonverbally usually wins the day!)*

Sounds simple. Is simple. And it's extremely effective to boot. I like to call it the "Ladder of Flattery" because when you use these six simple steps in any conversation, the person with whom you're speaking is bound to walk away with a smile on her face, thinking, *Now, that is one nice person, and what a great conversationalist!*

Don't be too proud to use the Ladder technique to ensure that your dialogue doesn't degenerate into a one-way street, with all of the traffic coming from your direction. How can you effectively empathize with a person when you have the pedal to the metal and you're blasting by them at full speed?

Too often we depress the walkie-talkie button far too long. Let go and listen!

It's human nature to tune out the other person while we wait for our turn to talk. We talk *at* each other, not *with* each other. But think of what you're missing: the person you're not really listening to might happen to have a cool idea, a clever suggestion, or even a plan for a better mousetrap.

Being a good listener is also a great gift for anyone who aspires to be accepted, well liked, and respected. That's because people are naturally drawn to the person who shows a genuine interest in them.

Bartenders and hairstylists who are good listeners get the

biggest tips. Dates who are good listeners become marriage material. Friends who are good listeners become best friends. CEOs who are good listeners stay on the cutting edge—a not-so-easy feat.

Besides being a charming trait in others' eyes, good listening skills are also valuable to you as the listener. The more you talk and the less you listen, the less you learn. You already know what you know, and so constantly speaking your own thoughts won't expand your mind. Now find out what someone else knows. Listening with a leader's eye requires restraint, respect, and a genuine dose of curiosity.

The curious thing about ideas is, you never know where or when one will happen along. Just by listening, you're apt to stumble across some beauties. Yogi Berra said, "You can observe a lot just by watching." Well, you can hear a lot just by listening, too.

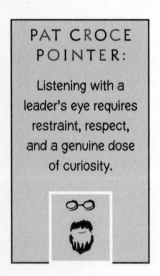

PAT CROCE POINTER:

Listening with a leader's eye requires restraint, respect, and a genuine dose of curiosity.

THAT'S A SLAMMIN' IDEA!

Original thinking can blossom anywhere. Some successful business executives will tell you that some of the best recommendations have come from stock boys and desk clerks. Yet those who are further down the ladder of responsibility are rarely consulted; rarely are they invited to offer their opinion. But when they are included, they're grateful, and their ideas are often dead-on because they're around the public—the customer, the consumer—and understand what people really want.

They're in the trenches, and they have a different awareness of daily operations than you do. It's your loss if you, as the boss, do not seek their input.

One of my most recent and rewarding business ventures has been my involvement in the first extreme team sport: Slamball. You may have caught some of the hard-hitting, high-flying, slam-dunking action on Spike TV (formerly the TNN channel) on Monday and Saturday nights. If not, you should. It's wild!

Slamball is identified by its fast-paced four-on-four action, which takes place on a revolutionary, heavily modified, spring-loaded basketball court with four regulation-size trampolines built into the court at either end, surrounding the baskets. To make the game more conducive to full-body collisions, the court is enclosed with a hockey-rink-style Plexiglas wall.

There is no out-of-bounds, and there are very few stops in the action. The top of the backboard—traditionally out-of-bounds—is even fair game in this sport!

Slamball players are padded from head to knee and look like warrior skateboarders. Powered by the trampolines, the athletes display such intense in-air maneuvers en route to the basket that they make Michael Jordan's antics look human. And their raw enthusiasm for the new sport is contagious.

It's a wildly entertaining sport, and to date has been a successful venture. I've enjoyed every aspect of my participation in this extreme creation. And without fail, fans and friends all want to know the same thing: "Where the hell did this idea come from?"

My answer: "From an intern!"

Mike Tollin, who runs the very successful Tollin/Robbins Production Company with his partner, Brian Robbins, is a great friend and an extraordinary leader. Together, Mike and Brian have earned due respect in Hollywood for producing such hit television shows as *Smallville* and *Arliss*, as well as movies like *Radio*, *Hardball*, and *Big Fat Liar*, and successful radio programming.

Mike gladly attributes much of his success to his practiced skill of attentive listening. The special quality of Mike's listening skills is that he does not reserve his nonfiltered ears for the words of screenwriters, investors, agents, directors, and movie stars. He also lends them to secretaries, interns, and even fans of his work!

One of his interns was a charismatic, athletic twenty-five-year-old named Mason Gordon. Mason approached Mike with an outrageous idea for creating a new team sport for television that would appeal to an eager generation of action-oriented, nontraditional athletes. The stroke of lightning in a bottle that led to Mason's thunderous idea was his attentiveness to the stunning success of ESPN's X Games and NBC's Gravity Games, as well as the news-making potential inclusion of snowboarding in the upcoming Olympics. Clearly, in Mason's tuned-in mind, possibilities abounded. He began to develop ideas. And his ideas began to take shape.

Mike listened. Mason persisted. Mike asked questions. Mason was more than happy to answer them. Mike eventually decided that he liked the idea, and the rest is history. But if Mike had early on decided that his ears were too good for an intern's "insignificant" opinion and suggestions, the concept of Slamball might have been history.

KEEP YOUR FINGER
ON THE PULSE

Of all employees, the ones with whom the public most often deals are the secretaries—at least twice a visit. I was told a long time ago that they are our windows to the world. And so they are equipped with a unique perspective on the pulse of the people. It is only logical that their input should be actively sought and encouraged.

When I expanded the Sports Physical Therapists centers, I used our secretaries' suggestions when building the secretarial suites—the axles on which our wheels turned. We met regularly to share information. After all, if you want to know how the battle is going, who better to ask than the ones who are on the front lines? That's not a thing you learn if you're in the corporate suite and never come downstairs.

As president of the Sixers, I literally moved out of a gorgeous corporate suite in the Comcast-Spectacor executive offices located in the First Union Center in order to get closer to the pulse. These offices were reserved for the corporate staff that oversaw the management of the Philadelphia 76ers and Flyers, the First Union Center and the First Union Spectrum, and other related corporate entities.

This exclusive area of the building housed offices that were designed by professional space planners and furnished by artsy interior decorators. They were the kind of offices that had large floor-to-ceiling windows, not to mention a ton of other impressive amenities. Yet they were three floors above the rest of my Sixers staff.

My team—both the business side and the basketball side—had offices on the event level of the First Union Center, on the same floor as the locker rooms and basketball court. There wasn't an ounce of sunlight streaming through those walls, but there was a thousand pounds of energy and laughter streaming through the hallways.

I felt that I needed to be where the action was. So I relocated to a small but comfortable office in the core of activity.

And my office sported a great location. Every staff member had to pass my open door if he was traveling to or from the basketball court.

I knew from experience that often the best flow of information, not to mention the best flow of fun, could be found in the office hallways. They are also the best locale for plucking news from the grapevine and for finding reasons for recognition and celebration. And you definitely don't require a phone call or an appointment to get in on the flow of action.

I've always been effective by following the concept of "MBWA"—Manage By Walking Around. And my staff enjoyed my dropping by to inquire: "What's the progress on . . . ?" "What do you think about . . . ?" "Are you up to speed on . . . ?" "How's the family enjoying . . . ?" In fact, Dave Coskey, our vice president of marketing, would liken my bouncing from office to cubicle to office to a human pinball, with all of its energy and commotion.

Speaking of those corporate suites, there's a certain piece of hardware that ought to be done away with, regardless of the floor number:

The door.

Doors exclude. And one of the successful secrets of leadership is to *include*. You shouldn't want to keep people and ideas out; you should want to invite them in.

A closed door suggests a closed mind. A closed door is a form of alienation. A closed door shouts: *Stay Out!* A closed door suggests you are doing, saying, or thinking something you don't want anyone to know or hear. But what's most damaging, a closed door tells your employees to keep their thoughts to themselves.

And what if they have some really good ones? They'll remain on the other side of your door, away from your ears and out of your reach. So, keep doors open. Better yet, get rid of them altogether.

In the art of listening like a leader, think of closed doors as earplugs.

I value the input of my staff so much that I created a system to keep the lines of communication open and active. It's called the "Five-Fifteen," and I recommend it to any leader. I've used it successfully in all of my business endeavors.

Every Friday, all employees, managers, and everyone else right up through the vice presidential level write up a progress and activity report that lands on their supervisor's desk. Eventually, all the information trickles up to me.

The idea is that the report takes five minutes to read and fifteen minutes to write. Hence, "Five-Fifteen."

The Five-Fifteens serve two main purposes: they keep practical information flowing, and they get the celebrations going.

Not only do employees write about responsibilities they are handling and goals they are striving toward, they also have the chance to brag about accomplishments and gloat about victories great and small. No one thinks of the Five-Fifteens as a chore, but rather as a chance to steal the spotlight on a Friday afternoon.

I love them because they help me keep my finger on the pulse, and they give me an opportunity to single out individuals for a job well done.

And compliments are like investments that pay instant dividends.

THE DAFFODIL PRINCIPLE

Since I have never assumed that the intent of my words always makes its way through the labyrinths inside my staff's ears, I've shared the Daffodil Principle with them to tug on the inner chambers of their hearts.

The Daffodil Principle was first published in a book entitled *Celebration* by Jaroldeen Asplund-Edwards. It's a colorful story that touches on the problems that follow when you hear but do not listen. Its moral is that when you don't pay attention, there is usually regret. But if you're lucky, there is redemption. It goes like this:

A daughter kept calling her mother, urging her to come and visit. They would go and see the daffodils together. But they'd have to hurry because the daffodils would soon lose their bloom.

The woman heard her daughter, but didn't really catch the urgency in her voice. Besides, it was a two-hour drive, which she'd be making soon enough anyway. She wanted to see her daughter, but . . . You know how it is.

Still, the daughter kept calling, kept pestering. The woman kept hearing the voice, but not the emotion.

Finally, she agreed. "I'll come next Tuesday."

Tuesday was dismal, rainy and cold. But the woman had promised. Besides, there would be a bonus—she would get to see her two grandchildren.

Upon arriving, she hugged her daughter and her grandchildren and drank some tea to get the cold out of her bones.

"Forget the daffodils," the woman told her daughter.

"Oh, but Mother . . ." The daughter thought quickly and said, "I was hoping you could take me to the garage to pick up my car. And I'll drive. I'm used to this weather."

"All right," the mother said.

So they set off. But after ten minutes it became apparent that the daughter wasn't driving to the garage.

"Where are we going?" the mother asked.

The daughter smiled. "We're going the long way—by way of the daffodils."

The mother grew stern and insistent. "Please turn around."

The daughter tried, one last time, to get her mother to understand. "You'll never forgive yourself if you miss this."

They drove on in silence. Finally, they came to a small gravel road. At the end, there was a hand-lettered sign: DAFFODIL GARDEN. Just beyond the sign was a path, and they set off. Very soon they turned a corner, and what the mother saw took her breath away.

The daffodils spread along the slopes like an immense rainbow. The flowers had been planted in majestic, swirling patterns across the slopes in glorious colors—lemon yellow, salmon pink and saffron, sunset orange, and a white so bright it made you blink.

"Who," she asked her daughter, "has done this?"

"The woman who lives here."

They approached a modest A-frame house that sat unobtrusively in the midst of all that splendor. On the patio was this poster: "Answers to the questions I know you are asking."

The first answer: "50,000 bulbs."

The second: "One at a time. By a woman. Two hands. Two feet. Very little brain."

The third, and last: "Began in 1958."

The mother's mind reeled at the scope of the project. One woman had spent half a century bringing to radiant life her vision of beauty and joy, spread out lovingly over a mountain meadow.

And she had done it one bulb at a time.

The mother thought of the times her daughter had spoken to her, and she hadn't really heard. And she felt a stab of sadness and regret, and of opportunity missed.

"I was just thinking," she said to her daughter, "what I could have accomplished by now if I had set for myself some goal fifty years ago."

And the daughter looked at her mother, smiled, and said: "Start today."

Sounds like beautiful advice to me.

SIX

Slay Them with Super Service

THE GOLDEN RULE

Do unto others as . . .

Oh, you know how it goes. The Golden Rule was one of the very first things you ever learned. And it's still the recommended way to approach every aspect of life: with compassion and tolerance, with patience and nobility of purpose, with consideration and genuine concern for your fellow man and woman. This is especially true when the men and women in question are invested in helping you achieve your vision. When practiced consistently, the Golden Rule pays off for anyone . . . and everyone.

For leaders, though, the Golden Rule is more than a recommended practice. It's a necessity. Because failing to live by those golden words is reputation suicide.

Of course, I like to take the Golden Rule and crank it up. Don't just do unto others as you'd have them do unto you; do unto others as you'd have them do unto you *in your wildest dreams!* Don't just provide service; *slay them with super service!* Go overboard. Turn over every stone. Do more than is expected, or even conceived. And apply these killer tactics to everyone from customers to employees to family to friends. The little extra you may have to put in will always earn out.

Fortunately, the magnitude of the Golden Rule's importance is complemented by its simplicity of execution. All you have to do, really, is think of how *you* would like to be treated in any given situation, and then act accordingly. Consider all those times you've played the role of customer, or partner, or employee, or volunteer, or intern, or student, or son or daughter; then consider how you *were* treated and how you *wished* you were treated by the person or people in charge.

There. Now you know, in theory, how to act. The next simple step is just to bring this theory into reality. But in reality, the first thing we learn about actually practicing the Golden Rule is . . . *Wow, is this hard or what!*

All our faults and weaknesses threaten to get in the way. Envy. Pettiness. Prejudice. Pride. Spite. Impatience. Greed. There isn't an easy way around them. So what you do is bite down and consistently keep on trying. And the more you try, the more it becomes a habit. And then it becomes part of your behavior. And then it becomes ingrained in your character. Which is an accomplishment for anyone when you consider that it is not in everyone's nature to do the right thing.

For example, I'm sure you've heard of the "other" Golden Rule, the one that's applied to business: *Do unto others before they can do unto you!*

It's funny, yes, but dripping with cynicism. It is the very antithesis of the original. Sadly enough, it's always had a place in the business world. But lately, such brutal and blatant disregard for others has become an epidemic among top business leaders.

All throughout the spring and summer of 2002 and beyond, the "other" Golden Rule was exposed as the established mantra of corporate culture. And it took on an even more sinister definition: *He who has the gold makes all the rules.* Ethics took a beating. Greed was good. For months, every nightly newscast seemed to overturn another rock that would send the rats scurrying frantically for cover.

We were awash in corporate scandal, highlighted by a laundry list of leadership don'ts. Cooked books. Fraudulent reports to stockholders. Inflated earnings. Disappearing losses. Manipulated stocks. Executives either caught in lies or hiding behind the Fifth Amendment. CEOs bailing out and pulling the ripcord on their golden parachutes. Numerous declarations of bankruptcy and a disastrous desecration of trust.

And this loss of trust—which started at the top—has the potential to affect the public's perception of everyone in the business world. Which pretty much includes all of us. Still, through my rose-colored glasses, I see this dark time as an opportunity to embrace a brighter future . . . a more vivid vision. And to redefine what it means to be a leader.

A good place to start is by embracing the Golden Rule as your philosophy, and by practicing the "Ten Commandments of Service" that I developed for my staff (and myself!) at Sports Physical Therapists, used effectively in the resurrection of the

Philadelphia 76ers franchise, and continue to use in every enterprise that bears my name and spirit.

It's imperative to remember that I am a big believer in "servant leadership," where service to others creates an atmosphere and attitude for leadership of others. The Ten Commandments of Service are truly the backbone of my leadership technique.

You'll see that the concepts are simple; but if you dare embrace them, you'll see that they aren't so simple to apply. But the hard work and discipline you undertake to make these commandments law in your own life will bring surprisingly satisfying results. Not only will you firmly establish your leadership position in the minds of your staff, customers, family, and friends, but you will be setting an example for those who share your vision.

I have applied this ten-point strategy to all my businesses and civic endeavors, and even to my everyday life. It hasn't failed me yet.

THE TEN COMMANDMENTS OF SERVICE

1. Hello . . . and Good-bye

Hello.

And good-bye.

These are the basics in customer service, in human relations, no matter what your business. You greet the person with a hearty hello, and you bid her good-bye with equal vigor.

Even if you don't really mean it.

Think about all the times you've stood in line—at the bank, at the supermarket, at the post office, at the complaints department of any store. How are you usually greeted by the clerks, supervisors, and other staff? It's probably not an exaggeration to say that sometimes they treat you like you're something stuck to the bottom of their shoe.

Which is why a window-rattling, sincere "Hello!" is so effective. Especially when it's accompanied by a smile. This one-two punch suggests that you really care. It conveys that, for once, the person isn't just another number. Hello can be an attitude reverser, a tone setter, a stage setter, and an image creator.

I can state unequivocally that I have never entered my office, or one of my SPT centers, or the hallways of the First Union Center, or the lush ticket booths of our chain of Pirate Island miniature golf courses, or the set of Slamball, without giving a hearty hello to everyone I meet—employees and customers alike. I like to extend the same feeling that I get when I enter my home and feel the warmth of a friendly welcome from my wife, Diane, and our dog, Shemp (not always in that order).

I want my staff to feel good about my arrival. I want them to feel good about themselves. And I want them to extend that same enthusiastic attitude to all the customers and fans and peers they encounter. That's why I, as the leader, do it. Every day!

And every night!

During my five-year tenure as president of the Sixers, I never missed an opportunity to invest at least half an hour's worth of time on the arena's concourse every game night, greeting the concessionaires in their food stands and the fans in their jubilant mood as they entered the turnstiles prior to tip-off.

In addition to Sonny Hill, Philadelphia's Godfather of Basketball, I was accompanied by our community relations representative, the all-star, scintillating World B. Free, and several of the gorgeous ladies from our Sixers dance team. I wanted to make sure that the masses of fans received a hearty hello to kick off their evening's experience.

Good-bye is just as important. But it requires a little more discipline not to let people slink away undetected. Be sure that they leave with a heartfelt adios ringing in their ears. It's the impression of you and your endeavor that they will take out the door with them. It's how they'll remember you.

Leave them with a little extra. A little *Take this home with ya!*

Ultimately your greeting and send-off will have a definite effect on whether they'll be back again.

Hello. Good-bye. So simple. But then, what works usually is so, so simple.

2. First-Name Basis

There is no sound in the world as sweet as your own name. It is a form of vanity to which we are all innocently susceptible. It is the starting point of our very identity, the first thing that separates us from everyone else.

Which is why it is so important to conduct all your business and social interaction on a first-name basis.

As with hello and good-bye, calling people by name is a guaranteed way to make them feel important. Or at least feel that they're important to you. Which means that they'll readily choose your store, service, friendship, expertise, and leadership over those of others who don't offer such a personal touch.

If someone would rather be addressed by a title—Dr., Mrs., Reverend, Sister, etc.—then obviously, as with all matters, the customer (person) is always right. But my experience has been that people will react favorably to being called by their first name . . . especially those who look up to you as their leader.

And in my case, when I really get to know someone, I either use his existing nickname or christen him with a new one. This puts people in your inner circle and raises the bar of affection and respect—even when the nickname is seemingly sarcastic. Some of my best memories are stimulated when I hear the nicknames Fast Eddie, Rayman, Scramble Head, Hole, Hollywood, Bator, Bonz, Bobby Smiles, Aces, Amish, Spies, Stevie A, Stevie O, Slambro, Dude, Dougger, Marky Mark, Mack, Mutsi, Jakester, Jimbo, Punky, Princess, Gorgeous, Cochise, T-Bone, Meat, Mudman, Munchies, Sonny, Stretch, Greek, Shaggy, Snowman, and Bubba Chuck.

As the lyric in the theme song from the famous television show *Cheers* conveyed so perfectly: "Sometimes you want to go where everybody knows your name." Well, sometimes—or more likely, *all* the time—you want to follow someone who knows your name!

Using first names doesn't take much effort, and it offers great rewards. It also works both ways—whether you're running a business or patronizing one. When a clerk waits on you or a restaurant server first greets you, for example, simply notice her name tag and greet her by name. If there is no identification, ask her. Instantly creating a more intimate connection by using someone's first name is invaluable. It will usually guarantee you first-rate service, as it will definitely demonstrate that you care and value her existence. And you'll become a favorite, and favored, customer yourself.

Being a star player in the "Name Game" adds to your aura as someone who cares and is possibly worth listening to.

3. Listen. Listen. Listen.

Listening is an art. And an acquired skill. No one sets out to be a great listener, because human nature makes us want to be the one talking. But listening is the bedrock of leadership. It strengthens business relationships, personal friendships, family connections, and even encounters with strangers. Listening is the quickest, most accurate, and most effective way to understand people, and it gives you the info you need to react in a way that benefits both them and you. Creating this advantage is invaluable to a leader.

You listen with both ears, with a leader's eye, with open arms, and with every shred of gray matter you can summon. You listen, and if at all possible, you let others know just how carefully you are listening. This is done by making mental notes and then interjecting the occasional comment or question (but never as an interruption).

The simplest trick to becoming a good listener has nothing to do with your ears or your eyes or your brain; it has to do with your heart—you have to actually *care* about what others are saying.

When you truly care about another's concerns and thoughts and dreams, then listening becomes your pleasure. Not to mention your greatest asset.

One of my heroes is Madeleine Wing Adler. She is an educator and cancer survivor. A wife and scholar. A mother and pioneer. A confidante and friend.

And most definitely, a leader worth emulating—and following.

Since 1992 she has been the president of West Chester University (in the suburbs of Philadelphia), the first woman to hold that position. But then she is accustomed to swimming against the current. She was breaking ground and breaking down barriers well before the women's rights movement.

Her philosophy of leadership is to share her vision and involve everyone on her passionate team, not just an elite few. She sees her employees as experts in their own right, as unique sources of knowledge and experience and wisdom, and as the keys to implementing change for the better.

When Madeleine first arrived on campus, she set out on an inspection tour. This is no ivory-tower elitist who never ventures from the office. She manages by walking around (MBWA) . . . to the extreme!

During her first August there, for example, she visited the

boiler room. She was wearing a yellow linen jacket at the time, a choice she would regret later. But her point had been made: I'm here to see all of you, to see what you do and how you do it, and to find out what we can do to help you.

Leadership in the trenches. Listening to the front line.

Invariably the people she talked to would get around to asking her: "This is the problem, so what are you going to do about it?"

And she would answer: "I'm not going to do anything about it. But what I will do is help you figure out ways to resolve issues. And I say 'resolve' rather than 'solve' because not every issue can be solved. But most can be resolved."

In general, Madeleine is fond of asking the question "So what is your opinion?" And then attentively listening to the answer!

Everyone feels empowered and emboldened when they work for or with her. Perhaps the most striking example of the can-do climate she consistently fosters is West Chester University's relatively new policy about summer school.

It's free!

That is, the room and board are free for all full-time summer students.

The idea was first suggested, casually and almost in passing, by a campus manager. It was one of those *you-know-what-we-ought-to-try?* remarks that are invariably accompanied by a chorus of *yes-great-idea!* acceptance . . . and then promptly forgotten.

But this suggestion was really heard—by a really strong leader—and it stuck. A work team was formed. And the idea that had first been voiced in February had become reality by May. That's a phenomenal rate of progress in such a setting; usually bureaucracy will ensnarl a project in its tentacles and squeeze the life out of it.

Still, like many good ideas, approval was hardly unanimous.

Madeleine said: "When people first heard about what we were planning—*free* room and board—a few of them thought I had snapped. Others were thrilled.

"One parent said, 'Do you mean that my son can go to school all summer, you pay for his housing and his meals, and I don't have to live with him? Where do I sign?'"

The impact was immediate, and immediately favorable. Enrollment went up. So did revenues. So did morale. All because one leader's ears—and arms—remained open.

4. Communicate Clearly

Allow no margin for any "mis."

That is, misunderstanding, misinterpretation, or miscommunication.

There's an old saying that states, "While it might not seem like there's ever enough time to get a job done, there always seems to be plenty of time to do it over again."

The problem usually begins when someone misunderstands a direction, or misreads an order, or makes a mistaken assumption rather than asking a question. So be clear and concise whether you're giving orders or taking them. Whether you're communicating your feelings or listening to another bare his soul. Many people fail to completely clarify communication out of arrogance, shyness, laziness, or the mortal sin of making assumptions. None of which are acceptable when you're the leader.

Here's a fun little exercise—called "Do as I do"—that illustrates how bad the habit of *assuming* and jumping to conclusions can be. Challenge a staff member to do exactly what you do (it's a little like the game "Simon says" but without the words). Each of you picks up a glass full of water. You make a gesture with the glass as if you are toasting; and the other person follows your *salud* move. You take a drink of your drink; and the other person drinks his or hers. You perform the toasting gesture again; and the other person parrots the move. You spit your mouthful of water back into your glass; and chances are the other person has already swallowed his or her drink!

Complicated conversations raise many questions and, hopefully, provide many answers. So never shy away from them. And never shy away from asking questions instead of assuming directions. And finally, remember the one question that should always be asked and answered in every conversation: "Are there any more questions?"

In a business setting in particular, this question is the last thing a staff member or customer should hear from you. Well, right before your earnest and energetic "Good-bye."

5. Be Neat, Clean, and Fit

Grooming matters. Your appearance is the first impression you're going to make in every new situation, and since you never get a second chance to make a first impression, it's inevitable that this impression will stick in people's minds no matter how many subsequent impressions you get to take a crack at.

You don't need a million-dollar wardrobe or personal trainer to master this commandment. Just common sense, self-respect, and the time it takes to complete a regular workout, attend to personal hygiene, and maybe iron a shirt or blouse.

But the job isn't finished when you put on your Sunday best. Being neat, clean, and fit is an active occupation that requires constant attention. Slouch and slump, and you're hinting that you might be sloppy in your work and careless in your service. Carry excess weight that drags you down, and you'll not be taken seriously when you ask others to maintain a high energy level on the job.

Standing straight as a bayonet and being neat as a pin creates an air around you from which you exude confidence. And confidence breeds trust.

Fitness aside, I have always been a stickler about being neat and clean—probably learned in my early years from the backhand discipline of my father. But it worked! And it continues to work in everything I do and in every environment in which I work, from a neat desk to a clean garage. A tidy work atmosphere in any endeavor will help save you time and trouble while garnering a degree of respect from those who watch your every move. And don't be naive. As a leader, your actions, as well as your inactions, are being monitored and weighed 24/7!

6. Be Prompt and Professional

Time truly is money. But it is actually a more valuable resource than cold cash. For what is time, but life itself? You can't save time. You can't borrow time. You can't rewind time. And you don't know how much time you have left on this third rock from the sun. So I say spend it on being the best that you can be.

Don't waste time. We all have only a certain amount of it to play with—you, your family and friends, colleagues, and customers alike.

How you treat time—how you manage or mismanage it—reveals more about you to others than any of the honeyed words that might come oozing from your mouth when you're explaining why you were late.

Being on time is mostly a matter of self-discipline. Make yourself leave early for an appointment. Set the alarm ahead fifteen minutes. And when you promise a customer that you'll have his order filled at a specific time and date, then regard that as a deadline in the most literal sense of the word. The same sense of deadline should be set for all your pursuits, business or pleasure.

If you're in the habit of being late, then eventually customers, employees, and even friends won't have any more time for you or your vision. My employees always respected my ability to start and finish a meeting on time. No excuses! They appreciated that I respected *their* time. They knew that no meeting would ever last longer than ninety minutes. They knew that their calls and e-mails and faxes would be addressed in a timely fashion. And they knew my feeling, reinforced by the horrific events of 9/11, that there are no guarantees in this journey, so make this present time count.

In all situations, a leader must walk the talk. And adhering to your word regarding your time commitments is no exception. In fact, being on time happens to be one of the easiest ways to prove your word is gold and your rule is golden.

7. Be Positive

One of my favorite stories is about the little boy who comes downstairs on Christmas morning and finds a sizable pile of horse manure on the floor by the Christmas tree. Does he hold his nose? Back away? Cry? No, he says: "Oh boy . . . I just know there's got to be a pony around here someplace!"

Now that's positive thinking.

I think you can be both a realist and an optimist. Obviously things will go wrong. Shit happens! But do you notice how they seem to go wrong a lot more frequently if you're expecting them to go wrong?

I have come to realize that life has a way of becoming a self-fulfilling prophecy. So if you always expect the worst, you will hardly ever be disappointed. Well, my way of thinking is: why not vice versa?

Expect the best. Expect success. I believe our efforts tend to match our expectations. When you work on controlling your thoughts, you have a better chance of controlling your world. Don't let your thinkin' become stinkin'. Who wants to live in a smelly, stinkin' world anyhow? Think positive. Be positive.

Customers and staff alike will respond to, and relate to, positive people. So will friends and associates. When someone exudes an air and a manner that convince others that they can get the job done . . . Well, whom would you take your business to? Whom would you allow to lead you?

Give me that pony kid every time.

Unfortunately, sometimes you end up with the opposite of the pony kid. Jackasses, if you will. We all know that these people exist everywhere and in all walks of life. And if you've ever had the challenge of dealing with such a person, then you'll love this story. . . .

It was the summer of 2001. My wife, two children, and I took a two-week vacation to Italy, the home of my paternal ancestors. The first week was spent bicycling through Tuscany, and what quickly became evident about this land was that it was filled with repentant sinners—or legions of saints in training.

I say this because the landscape was dotted with churches. There was at least one in every village we visited. Sometimes there wouldn't even be a village, just a church suddenly materializing out of a vast olive grove.

One day we stopped for lunch in Reggello—famous the world over for its olive oil—where we met a man who was eager to try out his broken English. Over a glass of vino, he told us a tale of the village priest who had saved his community's Sunday services from certain collapse.

On a recent sunny Sunday, this priest walked out into his churchyard, looked around and smiled, and said a silent prayer of thanks for the blessings of the day. He inhaled deeply and gave thanks for the sweet fresh air, then exhaled and turned around to find . . .

. . . a corpse.

It was a dead jackass, lying there in the dust of the church-yard.

The priest summoned the police. The policemen dutifully investigated, then announced that they had found nothing. There was no evidence of foul play; the jackass had apparently expired of natural causes.

"But what do I do with the body?" the priest asked.

The police suggested that he call the village sanitation department because it specialized in such things.

The priest did as the police suggested, but the head of the sanitation department said that while, yes, such removal was his responsibility, he would first need authorization from the mayor. And, he added, it would be up to the priest to secure said authorization.

Hearing this, the priest frowned. For the mayor, as everyone knew, was a cantankerous and sour old soul and thoroughly disagreeable to deal with. People went out of their way to avoid him and his nasty, negative attitude.

But what choice did the priest have? There was the body of the jackass, lying in the sun and dust of the churchyard, and not smelling any better by the minute. And if it was not removed, then the odor would be pungent enough to test the deepest, most abiding faith of the most devout parishioners in the village. Surely, Sunday's services would have to be canceled.

So the priest said a prayer, maintained his positive attitude, and knocked upon the mayor's door.

The mayor's response was exactly what the priest had feared. He ranted and railed about being disturbed over such a trivial matter. On and on he raged, berating the poor priest.

Finally, in a voice dripping with disgust, the mayor asked the priest: "Why on earth do you bother me with this nuisance? Aren't you supposed to be the one who is in charge of burying the dead?"

And with this, the priest smiled sweetly and nodded his head. "Yes, Mr. Mayor, I am," he replied. "But first, I like to notify the next of kin."

8. Give Compliments

A compliment costs you nothing to give, but it's worth millions, and its effect and return can be beyond measure.

None of us are immune to being complimented, whether it's on our appearance, our efficiency, our ability, or our character. I don't mean some vacuous, insincere stab at flattery. Most people can see right through that bullshit.

But the sincere compliment, ahhh . . . it's smooth going down and the sweet aftertaste lasts and lasts and lasts.

Look for reasons to compliment the work of your team. Doing so is not only a viable and valuable form of compensation, but it also serves as a natural incentive that inspires people to achieve even greater success and to seek the further compliments that come with it.

And be sure not to limit your praise to the major victories. Offer compliments liberally, and use them to recognize all levels of success. A great memo, a well-prepared meeting, and a creative solution to even a minor problem are all worth a quick shout of "Great work!"

After all, without the little achievements, your big goals don't stand a chance.

Once you realize that everyone, and I mean *everyone*, wants to feel valued, feel appreciated, feel important, then you will better understand the value of this underutilized commandment.

Imagine the look on your child's face after you compliment her on the coloring-book picture that she just colored and how well she stayed within the lines of the drawing. Marvelous! Beautiful! Great job!

Did you picture her face? The beaming smile? The attentive glow? The change in body language? The desire to do it again . . . and even better this time? Well, we never lose that childhood craving for attention and praise and a salute to our worth. Share the gift of a compliment.

There's a simple two-word maxim that sums it all up so well: "Praise pays."

9. Have Fun

We get so caught up in our work and in other responsibilities that all too often we forget to have any fun. Yes, a work ethic is most admirable. But so is a fun ethic.

A sense of humor will smooth out some of the bumps, fill in some of the potholes. As the saying goes, "laughter is the best medicine." In fact, a hearty laugh really is therapeutic. Laughter releases endorphins in your body that physically impact your emotional state for the positive. The simple act of forming a smile on your face — even if you do so for no reason — actually and instantly puts your mind in a better mood. Try it right now. . . .

See what I mean?

I've always felt that a smile could kick-start the body and mind into a better mood. But when I read *The Tipping Point* by Malcolm Gladwell, I literally smiled and shouted with joy to find that this best-seller backed up my joyous beliefs.

Gladwell explained how the expressions on our face are a re-flection of our inner state. He described our emotional pathway as being *inside-out,* as reflected in the simple statements "I'm happy inside, so I smile," or "I feel sad inside, so I frown." Then he revealed the surprising news that psychologists now say that an *outside-in* emotional pathway is also viable. In other words, if I make you smile, I can make you happy. And if I make you frown, I can make you sad.

So smile, even if you have to fake it till you make it!

You'll also find that others appreciate it when someone—a leader in particular—smiles and finds the humor in a discomforting situation. Keeping a sense of humor can do more to ease tensions and move things in the right direction than panicking, sounding an alarm, and pandering to everyone's fears and apprehensions.

These qualities work wonders among all people. Encourage your employees and associates to smile, to be loose and relaxed, and to enjoy what they're doing. Atmosphere and attitude go a long way toward improving efficiency and morale.

And don't forget to celebrate—both small victories and large triumphs.

10. Do It Now!

Know what the most overused excuse in business is?

"Tomorrow."

I'll get around to it tomorrow. It's on my to-do list for tomorrow. Call you back first thing tomorrow. Promise.

Any of those clichés sound familiar? Of course they do, because we've all used them and had them used on us. But my belief is that tomorrow is one day too late. I like to take the famous Nike slogan—Just Do It—and add a slight twist. Just Do It *now!*

It is a practice and an approach that will separate you from the rest of the pack in a hurry. In business, for example, the way to win customers, keep customers, and get customers to recommend you to other potential customers is to give them service at warp speed.

The satisfied customer is the one who knows you'll be returning his phone call, answering her e-mail, responding to his correspondence . . . and that you'll be doing it *before* tomorrow. Most times, tomorrow is too damn late!

As famous oilman and business leader T. Boone Pickens said: "Be willing to make decisions. That's the most important quality in a good leader. Don't fall victim to what I call the 'Ready . . . aim . . . aim . . . aim . . . aim syndrome.' You must be willing to fire."

And once your decision has been made, you should waste no time in pulling the trigger.

My boyhood buddy Steve "Little Stevie" Stefano is a senior executive with GlaxoSmithKline (GSK, the second largest pharmaceutical company in the United States). He and his team were charged with the goal of developing a practical solution to the complex issue of providing access to medicines for needy senior citizens.

The fact is, there are approximately 11 million Medicare patients (sixty-five years and older) who do not have prescription drug coverage. It's amazing and sadly ironic that there is such negligible drug coverage for the people who need drugs the most.

In the summer of 2001, within just three months of accepting this exciting challenge, Stevie and his team launched their revolutionary answer: the GSK Orange Card (orange being GSK's corporate color). The Orange Card provided access to discounts at pharmacy counters across the country for all of GSK's products to all of those needy grandparents and other seniors.

The GSK Orange Card was a resounding success for the company. It was loved by the press. Applauded by the politicians. Embraced by the senior citizens themselves. And eventually copied by many of GSK's competitors.

Stevie told me that in his twenty-two years he was with the company, no experience has been more gratifying than the privilege of leading the Orange Card team to the fulfillment of its mission to serve the most deserving demographic in their industry—and to do so with a sense of urgency.

When you urgently serve others, attack problems, enact solutions, and express your sense of family and friendship, the rewards will come back to you with equal speed.

So what are you waiting for?

Right now is the best time to lead the charge and check off one more action step toward the realization of your vision.

A HOLE IN ONE!

When a comedian really nails his act—pulling out all the stops, delivering his absolute best in content and energy, and putting the audience in stitches—they say that he "killed 'em."

When I talk about "slaying them with super service," this same complete commitment to satisfy is in full effect.

For a long time now I've been involved in business ventures with an entrepreneur named Mark "Marky Mark" Benevento. We own and operate a franchise of miniature golf courses. You probably know the game as "putt-putt," but our courses are much bigger, cooler, and more adventurous than any normal putt-putt!

Pirate Island is what we call them, and they dot the South Jersey shore, a summer vacation hot spot. The business satisfies my consuming interest in the rebels of the sea, and it gives Mark an outlet for his creativity and love of all things golf . . . not to mention the courses being good real estate and business ventures.

Years ago, for research purposes, Mark went to Myrtle

Beach, South Carolina—an area that is covered with all styles of golf courses. He played them. He videotaped them. He pried loose all the secrets about design, management, and maintenance. Like me, Mark dotes on detail. You take care of the little things, and the big things will take care of themselves.

The detail in our courses is remarkable—and memorable. Our business has grown tremendously because of it, and we presently average between 250 and 300 rounds per course per day. And believe me, our miniature golf courses have come a long, long way from the days of the windmill and the clown's mouth.

There's a forty-foot suspension rope bridge, for example. And a forty-foot replica of a pirate ship. And caves. And fog machines that not only are cool but cool you, too. There are motion sensors. And Disney-like animatronics. And a rainbow of lights and sounds.

Plus waterfalls. And all sorts of rocks and cliffs. And a pool/water hazard—into which balls unhappily and often go. Followed, happily, by the players! We encourage such shenanigans because it adds to the experience.

In other words, it's not just about putting a colored ball into a hole. It's a sporting challenge. And it's an adventure to be shared and remembered.

As Mark has discovered, customer service, like employee service, can be boiled down to two words:

Listen and React—with action!

We have employees who are on constant walkie-talkie patrol. They monitor the traffic flow and the course cleanliness, and they're there to hear complaints and answer questions. You don't just throw open the door, hand people a putter and a ball, and then forget about them. Well, you can. But that's inviting well-deserved disaster.

One complaint Mark heard via the staff was the lack of a chance to win a free game at the eighteenth hole. We initially thought that the experience of playing the eighteenth hole on board a large replica of a pirate ship would be a great way to end the round of golf. But customers wanted their cake with icing.

So Mark devised a combination pin-ball/treasure-chest layout that enables the player to play all eighteen holes and then shoot for that coveted free game with a glorious hole in one.

In addition to the customers' voices being heard, our staff felt appreciated and encouraged because their voices had the power to make a difference.

PAT CROCE POINTER:

Customer service can be boiled down to two words: Listen and React—with action!

SHORT CIRCUIT TO SUCCESS

As a longtime business owner, I have always believed the axiom "The customer is always right." Why? Because I know that she has the discretion to spend her hard-earned money elsewhere. This is common sense, right?

Wrong! Plenty of business owners and managers treat their customers as if they were an obstacle, or even an enemy. And whenever I hear about this marketing method in action, I'm left speechless. But I'll try to untie my tongue for a minute to tell you about a surreal scene.

At the end of every summer, Marky Mark and I cook up a minigolf tournament and pizza party for the staff of all our Pirate Island courses. Most of our employees are high school and college students with a knack for having fun and a nose for free food. This is their day in the sun.

To show our gratitude for a summer of hard work and play, we end the party by giving each employee the choice of a really cool piece of electronic equipment—perfect for dorm rooms and bedroom hangouts. The order of choice is based on tenure, but even the most recent hire leaves hugging a prized new possession. It always electrifies me to see these great kids end each season with expensive new toys.

Last summer, Mark and our big-boned buddy Ralphie performed the ritual "supermarket sweepstakes" tour in an electronics superstore. In no time flat they had three shopping carts overflowing with DVD players, MP3 players, television sets, monster boom boxes, and minicomponent hi-fi systems. It was Christmas in August.

Suddenly, a store employee appeared and asked if he could be of any assistance. Mark shook his head and happily said, "No, thanks. We're cool. Everything's completely under control." He and Ralphie were having way too much fun selecting gifts and anticipating the expressions on the recipients' faces. (I love how, as you get older, giving gifts becomes more fun than getting them!)

The store employee then asked, with an air of indignation, "What do you think you're doing taking all this equipment off the shelves?"

Dumbfounded, Mark replied, "Buying it!"

"You can't do that," the irritated employee said. "You have to fill out a form, and we'll order it for you. We don't want to lose our inventory."

My buddies were stunned. Mark asked, "Can you get the store manager?" He threw a look toward Ralphie as if to say, *Can you believe this clueless clerk?*

"I *am* the store manager," the man replied.

"Oh," Mark said, now utterly confused. "So, as the manager

of this store, you're telling us that this stuff is for sale, but we can't buy it."

"That's right."

Mark considered the problem for a moment. He conjectured as to what, exactly, would prevent this guy from wanting to ring up several thousand dollars in sales. And all he could think of was the possibility that the superstore manager must have thought that Mark and Ralphie were purchasing the items for resale at a higher price and at the competition's store.

So Mark informed the man that the items weren't being purchased for resale, but were to be the highlight of an employee party. He described the golf courses, and the great employees we have, and even the looks on the kids' faces when they open their prizes.

No luck there.

But luckily for the misguided manager, Ralphie didn't squeeze his warped head into a portable microwave oven.

Instead, Mark asked one more question to give the man one last chance to do a brisk $3,500 worth of business. "What if I brought a busload of young customers to your store and directed each of them to purchase one of these items—on me—would that be okay?"

"Sure," the store manager replied.

"Well, just imagine that they're waiting in the parking lot and we're doing the buying for them!"

Again, no luck. And no clue.

Shaking their heads, Mark and Ralphie turned and left the store manager stranded with three shopping carts filled with items to be reshelved.

Minutes later, when Mark stepped into the competition's store, he asked to see the manager. "Can I buy anything and everything I want in here?"

The man looked at Mark as if he were nuts, and replied, "Yes. Of course."

Mark thanked him and pushed Ralphie in the direction of the shopping carts.

Our employees are still smiling.

ONE-OF-A-KIND
SPECIAL DELIVERY

The most important point I can make in this chapter is that a leader's commitment to service should not begin and end with the customer or client. It must encompass everyone!

I've always believed in trying to make each customer, each employee, each fan, each person, feel special. And that's what we did when the 2000 Republican National Convention was held in Philadelphia.

Through a few fortuitous relationships—and ultimately a special phone call from my friend and a man I admire, Comcast president Brian Roberts—I was recruited to be the volunteer chairperson and to help recruit the volunteers who would be necessary to make such a massive undertaking possible.

Shortly thereafter, a woman named Alison Grove, the director of community outreach for the nonpartisan and nonprofit host committee called Philly 2000, put her steely grasp on me and never let go.

Alison is a blond dynamo and she gets right to the point. During our first conversation, Alison made her pitch.

"I don't even have a short list," she told me. "You're it, and that's it."

How could I say no? The eyes of the world would be focused

on our city, the event would be great for the local economy, and, according to Alison, it would be tons of fun.

I should have asked her to clarify "fun."

Alison is an organizing whirlwind. She figured we'd need ten thousand volunteers to make the convention work. We ended up with eighteen thousand and actually deployed twelve thousand generous and gregarious men and women. It was a yearlong process.

After we had painted our vision, set goals, developed tasks, and prioritized our action steps, the action got hot and heavy.

Alison and I went from mall to mall, making public appearances to spread the word, and gathering volunteers along the way. We created and aired public service announcements. And since Alison knew I was game for promotional activities, and coincidently since the circus was in town, she had me climb an elephant and enlist it as a volunteer. After all, who's a more appropriate volunteer than the symbol of the Republican Party?

Getting people to commit to volunteer service is not, as you might imagine, as easy as, say, giving away free food and electronic gifts. So you have to paint the vision in Technicolor, offer all volunteers a sense of ownership, promise them a wonderful experience, challenge their civic duty, and then deliver on these promises.

Our approach was to treat the volunteers as though they were customers. We catered to them, and in turn they would cater to the delegates. But first we had to prepare them for service, knowing that if you fail to prepare, you're preparing to fail. We partnered with the Dale Carnegie program in order to get our volunteers ready for the convention. In all, there were forty-three training sessions, each one lasting ninety minutes. (Anything longer, and I would have vetoed!)

The volunteers were told to know their product (which, in this case, was the city of Philadelphia). Know the schedule. Know how to give directions, but not by speaking Philadelphian (for example, don't send someone to the "Schuylkill Expressway"; rather, direct them to the more recognizable "Route 76"). Be positive. Be on time. Speak clearly. Look good. Smile and be friendly. And treat each delegate as though he or she were a guest in your home.

From the core volunteers, including my daughter Kelly and my assistant Je'Juan, we selected a few hundred who were called Philadelphia Friends, and essentially they served as personal concierges to the delegates.

It all worked. The convention was a smashing success, and we sent thousands of people back home with smiles and fond memories of Philadelphia.

And we treated our volunteers to an amazing party at Penn's Landing, along the Delaware River. Most important, we held that party the week *before* the convention.

Sounds unusual, right? Not in my Golden Rule world. Because when I say, "Slay them with super service," I'm not only talking about the customers and clients; I'm also talking about the employees and staff. These individuals are your most important customers! They are buying your vision and goals and spreading your gospel and goodwill.

And we all know the most effective

> **PAT CROCE POINTER:**
>
> When I say, "Slay them with super service," I'm not only talking about the customers and clients; I'm also talking about the employees and staff. These individuals are your most important customers!
>
>

marketing strategy is positive word of mouth from a satisfied customer.

LIFTERS AND LEANERS

No matter how you serve your customers, staff members, teammates, neighbors, or others, you will surely develop a reputation based on your actions and your character. And those two things—your actions and your character—are completely in your control.

Here is a poem I like to recite that illustrates the basic choice a leader must make. Make the right choice, make it every day, and you will become a leader who is worth following.

Which Are You

by Ella Wheeler Wilcox

*There are two kinds of people in the world today,
Just two kinds of people, no more I say,*

*Not the good and bad, for 'tis well understood
The good are half bad and the bad are half good.*

*Not the happy and sad, for the swift flying years
Bring to each man his laughter and each man his tears.*

*Not the rich and the poor, for to count a man's wealth
You must first know the state of his conscience and health.*

*Not the humble and proud, for in life's busy span
Who puts on vain airs is not counted a man.*

No! The two kinds of people on earth I mean
Are the people who lift and the people who lean.

Wherever you go, you will find the world's masses
Are ever divided in just these two classes.

And strangely enough, you will find, too, I ween
There is only one lifter to twenty who lean.

This one question I ask: Are you easing the load
Of overtaxed lifters who toil down the road?

Or are you a leaner who lets others bear
Your portion of worry and labor and care?

SEVEN

Celebrate the Journey

Some people rationalize that "the ends justify the means." In other words, as long as things turn out okay, then whatever happens along the way is acceptable and even forgettable. People have been known to apply such pretzel logic to everything from running a business and raising a family to winning at any competitive endeavor.

Of course, they're missing out on half the fun.

I believe people sometimes just don't want to take responsibility for their actions when getting from Point A to Point B. I'm not talking about legal or moral responsibility here (two vital leadership qualities, no doubt); I'm talking about the responsibility of making the most of every moment and smelling the roses along the way, every day.

What's the point in getting from one place in life to another unless you enjoy the getting there? As far as I'm concerned, no journey is ever complete unless it has been worth the going. And in order to make all your *ends* in life actually mean something, you'll have to ensure that all your beginnings and middles mean something, too.

So enjoy the moment. Embrace the excitement. Celebrate

the journey. And seize the day. Or, as I like to say, "Carpe the diem!" (I throw the "the" in there for extra emphasis.) Because each action step you take and make happen is valuable in and of itself.

Some goals, visions, and ambitions, after all, result in failure. Or to put it nicely, they don't end up the way we plan them. Should this mean that all your efforts ought to be forgotten? Not if they were appreciated on their own merits.

I opened this book with an excerpt from the farewell speech I gave when I left the role of president of the Philadelphia 76ers, noting that I had walked away from leading the organization before realizing the final goal of a championship parade. But to this day, I believe the experience of that thrilling five-year journey would not have been as enjoyable and exciting had we not expected to ultimately live the vision and win it all. And had we not celebrated the little victories and momentous occasions along the way.

As the leader of the Sixers' band of rogues—which in my mind included everyone from players, coaches, staff, and management to the local media and especially the fans and customers— I took it upon myself to instigate much of the celebrating along the way. That's a leader's job. Whether I was involved in staging wild rallies, climbing local bridges to hang giant Sixers banners, preparing awesome giveaway nights for the fans, or even staging a Valentine's Day halftime wedding for seventy-six happy couples, I was always looking to

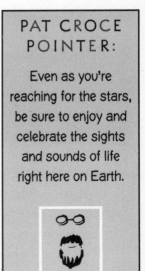

PAT CROCE POINTER:

Even as you're reaching for the stars, be sure to enjoy and celebrate the sights and sounds of life right here on Earth.

keep the smiles coming. And my staff never let me down with their ideas, inspiration, and dedication.

Even as you're reaching for the stars, be sure to enjoy and celebrate the sights and sounds of life right here on Earth. You'll be pleased to discover that your enlightened and enthusiastic attitude will be contagious among those who share your vision.

And you'll see that all those shared smiles will inspire you all to go that extra mile.

CELEBRATION EDUCATION

During staff meetings of all my past business and civic ventures, and within all of my motivational speeches and leadership seminars, I constantly stress the importance of celebrating. I beat people over the head with this concept like a child taking swings at a piñata!

Why? Because that's where the goodies are . . . packed inside each moment we take to celebrate.

Yes, I know the concept of "celebration education" seems a bit strange. To some, it may sound downright idiotic. You might even be thinking: *Who in his right mind doesn't know how to celebrate?*

But just think about this: When was the last time *you* celebrated? When was the last time you found yourself hooting and hollering, hugging, high-fiving, and head-butting your fellow travelers along the journey? When was the last time you found yourself throwing your arms in the air, striking a pose, and screaming, "Yes!" with the exuberance of a kid who just learned that school was canceled for the day?

If it's been a while, I have one more question for you:

Why?

When you're the leader, you must be ever aware that the focus and attention of your team is always on you. Your moods and attitudes are contagious, both the good and the bad. Fortunately, the ability to shape your mood is always completely in your control. Accentuating the good and reveling in the positives is a *choice*, nothing more. Conversely, focusing on the bad and dwelling in negativity is also a choice. And make no mistake about it: your choice in this matter sets the tone for every individual who stands behind you.

Little celebrations offer a big opportunity to set a positive, enthusiastic tone. So don't wait: celebrate! I believe it's great to have an end—a vision—to define your journey. But it's more memorable to thoroughly enjoy the journey in the end.

> **PAT CROCE POINTER:**
>
> Where morale and your belief system are concerned, numerous small successes count just as much as the rare big success.

As the great baseball promoter Bill Veeck said: "Every day is opening day."

Make a phone call to say "Great job!" or "Congratulations!" to a triumphant family member. Send a card or bouquet of flowers to a helpful friend. Slip a gift certificate into the hand of a deserving employee.

It has been found that where morale and your belief system are concerned, numerous small successes count just as much as the rare big success. And celebrating these moments really drives the point home. So if you think of yourself as a praiseworthy winner when little victories arise, then your mind-set will be more optimistic when the big challenges arrive. The act of savoring the small achievements is no small potatoes. In fact, each little victory is a stepping-stone toward a larger, grander success.

If you're lacking ideas for how to celebrate, try one of my three favorite methods:

1. Stretch for Success

One of the goals of this book is to reveal ways that you can figuratively stretch your time, talents, experiences, relationships, and leadership abilities to create greater success.

The Stretch for Success, though, is literally a physical stretch. It's designed to engage your entire mind and body in an action that engenders and envisions achievement.

At times, I ask my audience at talks and seminars to stand and perform the Stretch for Success because, as I stated in the first chapter of this book, "if you want to move people emotionally, then you must move them physically."

So I would like to ask you, the reader, to stand up! Please.

Now raise your hands into the air. Interlock your fingers. Rotate your palms toward the ceiling, straighten your elbows, and push your palms up to the stars. Be sure to breathe slowly—in through your nose and out through your mouth. Hold this position for ten slow beats, breathing deeply throughout, and then relax, keeping your hands above your head. I repeat: Do Not Hold Your Breath!

Gently release your intertwined fingers and rest your right hand on your left shoulder. With your left hand, grasp your right elbow. Slowly pull with your left hand, pushing your right hand off your shoulder and down onto your upper back. Now you are in the perfect position to pat yourself on the back.

That's right. Pat yourself on the back!

Feels good, doesn't it? I know you're smiling. And maybe you're even muttering about how easily I manipulated you into performing this exercise.

Well, it's about time!

I want you to get used to that tactile stimulation, that positive sensation, that wonderful realization that you have been, will be, and *are* a success. And I want you to feel that you deserve success and congratulations. On a daily basis, I would ask you to probe for reasons to pat yourself on the back, to celebrate more frequently.

And always remember: A pat on the back is only a few inches higher than a kick in the butt!

2. Strike a Pose

Madonna made the phrase "Strike a pose" famous in her video for the song "Vogue." Her three-word command compelled the black-clad dancers around her to contort their bodies into one provocative dance posture after another. If the goal was to look and feel sexy, it worked.

But I like to apply the expression "strike a pose" to the one singular stance that works for me in every celebratory occasion, large or small.

When the situation arises—which is just about every day—I am always fully prepared to strike a pose. As the urge hits, I immediately imitate the jubilant image of the winning athlete—arms extended above the head with hands balled into fists and a smile creasing my face from ear to ear. (Check out the cover of my book *I Feel Great and You Will Too!*)

Basically, when I "strike a pose," I look like the *Rocky*

statue that stands outside Philadelphia's First Union Spectrum.

You know it: it's the pose that Sylvester Stallone's character Rocky Balboa struck when he tore up the steps of the Philadelphia Museum of Art and completed his extraordinary training session. He achieved something remarkable, and he reveled in his accomplishment. I related to that moment, and so I adopted the pose as my own. It just feels natural.

But that's just me. Poses, like personalities, can come in many positions, postures, styles, and stances.

What is your pose of success? What do you do when you are really excited about something? What posture do you assume when you win a big game or close a big deal?

What are you thinking when you strike that pose? What are you feeling when the urge hits to express your excitement? What are you saying to yourself when you strike your pose? What do you scream aloud at that magical moment?

If you're like me, it may sound something like: "Yessssss!"

I love preening and screaming "Yesssss!" when I've successfully achieved a goal, realized a dream, or beat a deadline. Sometimes my scream sounds more like a guttural "Yaaaaaa!"

Other times, though, I'm capable of a more articulate expression of success. I'm talking, of course, about my signature, eardrum-shattering yelp of "I feel great!"

What's probably my most memorable scream of celebration came at a press conference in the spring of 1996 in which the sale of the Philadelphia 76ers was announced to the sporting world. In attendance were media members from every conceivable outlet. The multiple microphones that jutted out from the podium combined to concoct a veritable alphabet soup, with the letters ABC, CBS, NBC, ESPN, TNT, and CNN prominently displayed at the center of the dais.

This moment was more than six months in the making. It

was the culmination of hundreds of phone calls, countless hours of meetings, and a bottomless well of commitment. It truly was the realization of a dream, and a slew of intensely exciting emotions that had been brewing for days.

When it became my turn to speak, I had nothing to say. That is, not until I struck a pose with my fists to the stars and let out a wolfman howl that caused dogs to bark and sports fans to smile for a hundred miles! Then I took a breath, grasped the edges of the podium, and repeated my signature line—"I feel great!"—at about a hundred decibels!

To this day, whenever Sixers fans yell my name from the streets of Philadelphia—"Yo, Pat!"—I strike a pose. This never fails to encourage them to smile, scream, imitate my pose, and, hopefully, to acknowledge the undeniable power and sheer fun of celebrating.

I celebrate not only when I've reached landmark achievements—like that momentous Sixers press conference, or when we were lucky enough to win the NBA draft lottery in 1996, or when our team won the NBA Eastern Conference championship in 2001— but also after all those little victories that I cherish.

It may seem silly or contrived, but just try it and you'll see how good it makes you feel. The physical act of pumping your arms combined with the release of a good guttural shout is like an exclamation point at the end of

> ### PAT CROCE POINTER:
>
> Every time you tap into your unique talents and/or help someone else win his battles in life, take a moment to consider your achievement. And, realizing that it is a magical moment, feel free to punctuate it with a special expression.
>
>

a sentence. And it makes a strong statement: "I have succeeded, I am happy, and I am not afraid to show it and share
it!"

Every time you tap into your unique talents and/or help
someone else win his battles in life, take a moment to consider
your achievement. And, realizing that it is a magical moment,
feel free to punctuate it with a special expression.

It's your moment, and it deserves your unique stamp of approval. Go for it!

3. Victory Journal

There are many tools available that help monitor your journey through life. Things like daily planners and diaries, report
cards and performance appraisals.

But let me suggest something new: a Victory Journal.

Like many professionals, I wouldn't think of starting my day
without glancing at my daily planner, reviewing my to-do list,
and calculating the achievement of my daily game plan. But
unlike most individuals, I supplement this preview with an end-
of-the-day *review* that makes all that work worthwhile. It's called
a Victory Journal, and I write in it almost every day.

The content of any Victory Journal should include a wide
range of topics. One page may feature exultant notes about the
culmination of a huge deal; another may simply contain a few
giddy words about a great workout with a friend in need of shed-
ding some stress; or a page can be dedicated to the details of
how you helped someone accomplish a strenuous task.

Feel free to record pleasant surprises, the receipt of thank-
you letters and pats on the back, the sharing of acts of kindness
and words of wisdom, and *anything* at all that demonstrates
your power to have a positive impact on the day.

Obviously, some victories are very subjective. And other victories are definitely objective. But as long as you perceive something to be a victory (and we all know that perception is almost reality), then it *is* a victory, and it deserves a place in your Victory Journal.

Like a photo album, your Victory Journal will become a great collection of snapshots of positive experiences, and a living reminder of your power to achieve. With such a clear record of all your daily wins, successes, and achievements, you will slowly build a strong foundation for success.

The Victory Journal can be especially useful when your thinkin' becomes stinkin' and your attitude has twisted and soured. Any committed optimist worth his weight in wisdom would admit that it's difficult to remain upbeat and positive when the critics and cynics are forecasting rain on your parade. In such times, one glance at the pages of your Victory Journal can be quite restorative. You quickly see that you *have been* a winner and realize that you *can be* a winner again. Success begets success, and the simple act of reading your Victory Journal should prepare you to make another journal entry!

Your Victory Journal entries need not be anything more than just a few keywords or simple sentences. The idea is to stimulate a mental reproduction of those special snapshots of success.

For example, one of my journal entries is nothing more than the printing of two letters: "DJ." But every time I look at those two letters, I'm reminded of an incredible experience I had and of the extraordinary feeling one can experience upon positively influencing another's life.

One day I received the following e-mail:

Dear Mr. Croce:

My name is Brian and I'm 10 years old and I live in Lansdale, Pennsylvania. My friend DJ is recovering from an operation on a brain tumor and he will be sick for a long time from his medicine to take away his cancer.

He just got home from the hospital. Can you call or visit him maybe when you are not that busy? DJ would love it so much and it would probably make him feel a lot better, too.

Your fan,

Brian Palm

A brain tumor. Oh boy. I was accustomed to treating injuries and to helping athletes rehab their broken bones and sprained ligaments. But a child with cancer of the brain . . . what could I do to help?

Well, I knew from experience that a phone call could sometimes provide a real emotional bracer. So my assistant, Susie, e-mailed Brian to get DJ's number for me.

I dialed it, and a woman answered. I asked to speak to DJ.

There was a pause, and then a voice, slightly muffled.

"Hi."

"Is this DJ?"

"Yes."

"Yo, DJ, this is Pat Croce."

"Really? It's really you?"

"Honest. And I'm calling to see how you're doing. Your buddy, Brian, e-mailed me and told me about your recent surgery."

"I'm feeling good," he replied.

His voice began to perk up and pick up.

"Are you back in school?"

"Not yet, but pretty soon."

The stronger his voice got, the stronger I felt. And I told him that he was my hero. I'd had surgery myself a short time ago, but only on a leg. . . .

"If they went into my brain, DJ, they'd have to spend the first hour just removing all the rocks."

He laughed, and that sound was as sweet as spring rain.

I asked him if he'd like to go to a 76ers game with his family as soon as he was able.

"I'd love to go to a game!"

We said our good-byes and I asked to speak to his mother. She sounded upset, like she'd been crying.

"Is this really Pat Croce?"

"Yes." I laughed.

"Pat, those are the first sentences DJ has spoken since his surgery, two weeks ago."

All the air went out of me. A chill ran down my spine. I felt exhilarated and humbled and grateful and mystified all at the same time.

DJ's mother, Linda Farrar, said that since the surgery his only communication had been one- or two-word responses to his family's questions. But the doctor had told them that as DJ's brain healed, his speech and eyesight and coordination *should* return. Whether it was magical, medicinal, or something of a miracle, I like to think that something as simple as a phone call had an effect.

On both of us.

Every one of us, each one, is capable of that. One little

phone call. One little pick-me-up. One little bracer. One little compliment. One little helping hand. One little pat on the back. You never know the extent of the effect. All you know is that some outreach is needed, and who better than you to give it?

In the words of Ralph Waldo Emerson: "You cannot do a kindness too soon, for you never know when it will be too late."

SHARING IN OTHERS' SUCCESS

As a member of the Philadelphia 76ers and the Philadelphia Flyers organizations over the last two decades, I've had the privilege and pleasure of joining a wide array of postgame victory celebrations.

I've always loved the atmosphere in the locker room after a big win. It's filled with the kind of positive vibes I thrive on. And I love the fact that anyone who watches sports can also experience this magic "live" through the TV cameras and later through the reporting of the journalists who fill the room. The simple act of celebrating together strengthens our sense of community, our camaraderie, and our cohesiveness in facing the next battle.

Some of the most electric moments of my life have been spent in the eye of these victory storms, watching with millions of other fans as our winning warriors celebrated their achievements inside the great arenas on South Broad Street.

Five miles north of this sports complex, though, I enjoyed a similar sensation—but in a markedly different setting—when I was invited to attend the Philadelphia Police Department's Ninth District awards ceremony on North Broad Street. It was an afternoon I won't soon forget, as I was reminded of how truly important it is to celebrate our work—and our lives—along the way.

The playing field of the Ninth District team covers approximately two square miles, from Lombard Street north to Poplar Street, and from Broad Street west to the Schuylkill River, including the lively areas of Restaurant Row, the Avenue of the Arts, and Rittenhouse Square. Each day, the permanent population of seventy-five thousand receives nearly a half million visitors, making it a busy and tricky turf.

> **PAT CROCE POINTER:**
>
> Celebrating together strengthens our sense of community, our camaraderie, and our cohesiveness in facing the next battle.

The men and women who protect this district are honored each year with a luncheon and awards ceremony in which commendations are given and special achievements are honored. But unlike professional sports, where the media serve up every detail for the hungry fans, the highlight reel of the officers' season was shared by only a roomful of family and friends. To my mind, it's an event that should be shown live throughout the city on all television networks, and videotaped for repeated viewing.

Prior to the ceremony, there were a lot of hugs and hellos and smiles and high fives. And even though I was just along for the ride, I could feel and relate to this tough team's deep feelings for each other. The excitement and anticipation were electric as we all filed into the hall.

Then the ceremony began. As each honored officer reached the podium, he stood at attention as his achievements were described—like ESPN's *SportsCenter* with a law-enforcement twist! Then citations and medals were awarded, salutes were exchanged, and joyous applause erupted.

With the reading of each citation, I shook my head in disbelief. Here were real-life warriors, battling robbers, gangsters, rapists, and murderers. Guns and knives instead of hockey sticks and elbows. Every game was a life-and-death battle; every win was a championship. And the season never ended.

I realized as I listened to these accounts of unsung heroism that I might not be capable of handling such stress on a daily basis. And I felt increasingly awed by those who do. While I knew that the special night was for this family of which I was not a part, the effect that their sense of pride and achievement had on me was undeniable. That's simply a tribute to the power of celebration.

After the awards were given out, I was able to meet some of the officers. When I congratulated them with handshakes and hugs, I couldn't help but compare the bulletproof shielding under their uniforms to the equipment worn by hockey players. The difference was that this armor protected lives, not just livelihoods.

And I was reminded that pads and pats on the back are not just for athletes. Even as we routinely share in the celebrations of those who play a game for a living, there are plenty of others around us whose efforts we should celebrate. And by doing so, we are celebrating ourselves.

A CAUSE TO CELEBRATE

The darkest, most intense moments are when leaders are needed most. It is in these times that a leader is called upon — or takes it upon himself — to impart strength, provide comfort, assure victory, and even find a cause to celebrate.

We all know that life is too short. And as of September 11, 2001, we all know that life promises us no guarantees. All the more reason to carpe the diem!

Like every American, I felt enormous shock and grief upon hearing the news of the devastation visited upon the World Trade Center, the Pentagon, and Flight 93 outside Pittsburgh, Pennsylvania. It is the kind of seminal event that will cause each of us to remember exactly where he or she was on that horrible morning.

I happened to be in the comfort of my home, having just moments earlier concluded a live remote radio interview on Philadelphia's 610/WIP. Seconds after my interview ended, the morning show was interrupted by a news report that an airplane had just struck one of the World Trade Center towers.

Immediately, I turned on the TV to witness the events first-hand. I called out to my wife. Within minutes, we watched what might have been an unfortunate airplane accident trans-form into a horrifying terrorist attack as the second plane crashed into the south tower. We were speechless, and could only hold each other in disbelief as the tragedy unfolded. Slowly, Diane released herself from my grasp and telephoned our two children, who were nowhere near Manhattan but whose voices had to be heard.

In the hours, days, weeks, and months since that morning, our country has faced a most challenging aftermath. The gruesome pictures have been burned into our eyes, the endless stories of personal loss have broken our hearts, and a sense of vulnerability has entered our homes. I didn't know how—or if— we could rise above such adversity.

As a committed optimist, I have al-ways been in search of the silver lining.

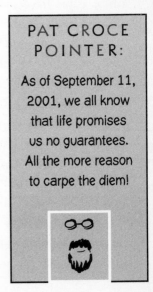

PAT CROCE POINTER:

As of September 11, 2001, we all know that life promises us no guarantees. All the more reason to carpe the diem!

And I relished and applauded the stories of all those heroes, small and large, whose deeds brightened our minds like a galaxy of shining stars throughout that very dark period.

I marveled at the silent efforts of the defiant passengers on Flight 93; the firefighter friar, Chaplain Mychal Judge, who died performing last rites on one of his brothers; the unyielding persistence and endurance of the firefighters, police, and emergency recovery personnel; the leadership of New York City's Mayor Rudy Giuliani; the tirelessness of thousands of unknown volunteers; and the millions of concerned individuals who donated money and/or time to the cause.

When I visited Ground Zero as a volunteer management member of the American Red Cross within the first week of the disaster, I encountered more than the immensity of the destruction. I saw hope and determination and courage and commitment and leadership.

Back home in Philadelphia, everyone was looking for answers as well as looking for a way to help. And sometimes, in strange times, as we have seen, an answer can take shape through the simple act of a phone call. This time, the call came *to* me.

My business manager and close friend, Steve Mountain, received a call on September 12 from a distraught friend, Sally Hyman. Sally was deeply affected by the horrific events of the previous day, and asked Steve to contact me in hopes that, together, we could do something to replicate the outpouring of pride and passion that the *entire* city of Philadelphia had generated three months earlier for the 76ers during our exciting playoff journey.

Sally, like many Americans, wanted to feel good again.

I eagerly jumped into the driver's seat and made a call to my friend Marc "Stretch" Cerceo, operations chief of the Philadelphia chapter of the American Red Cross.

In a matter of days (Commandment #10), the ball was rolling. With the creative support of Frank Donaghue (the chapter's exuberant president) and the rest of his American Red Cross team, the structural support of numerous corporations and media outlets, and the financial support of millions of caring citizens, Sally's idea was soon transformed into the tremendously successful "Raise a Million, Wave a Million" campaign. Simply put, the campaign called on everyone to make a donation and raise an American flag. Can you picture the vision? While we would be providing crucial resources, we would also be celebrating our country, our lives, and each other.

The press conference for the campaign was held just two hectic days later in Philadelphia's Love Park, across the street from City Hall. The park was jam-packed with thousands of individuals rallying for the cause. You could feel the tension in the air; it was a mix of sadness for what had happened, apprehension for what might come next, and a remarkable peace that seemed to originate in our collective, newfound desire to appreciate our shared journey through this sometimes torturous life.

Up on the star-spangled stage, in addition to numerous dignitaries representing the fields of politics, business, sports, and the arts, were our city's mayor, John Street; Philadelphia Eagles head coach Andy Reid; Philadelphia 76ers head coach Larry Brown; and the star of the show, Patti LaBelle, who sang the most soulful rendition of "God Bless America" I have ever heard. Tears ran freely in the crowd, and strangers offered hugs and pats on the back to each other.

As I stood there, I thought of the power of one woman's phone call. To this day, the positive chain reaction that started with that one call continues to touch the hearts and minds and souls of many.

In fact, just a few weeks after the initial "Wave a Million, Raise a Million" rally, I found myself standing on another stage, this time down on Columbus Boulevard near the Delaware River. The occasion was the unveiling of one of the most profound works of public art the city has known.

You can't miss the largest mural of the Stars and Stripes you have ever seen as you drive into Philadelphia from New Jersey or travel north out of the City of Brotherly Love on Interstate 95. The mural covers six thousand square feet, and represents the lives lost on September 11 in New York, Washington, and Pennsylvania.

Soon after our "Raise a Million, Wave a Million" campaign got under way, regional representatives of the Sherwin-Williams paint company had heard our public service announcements and called the American Red Cross. They had offered to memorialize the campaign—and honor and support those who were affected by the events of September 11—with an extraordinary American flag made of paint.

Two months later, this vast and vibrant symbol was unveiled.

And now it remains, a beacon of our resilience, a representation of our tragic loss, and a reminder that life has no dress rehearsal and each of us has a responsibility to celebrate the journey. And as a leader, it's your responsibility to lead the way in celebration.

In New York City, at the site of Ground Zero, there is a memorial banner that reads: THE HUMAN SPIRIT IS MEASURED NOT BY THE SIZE OF THE ACT, BUT BY THE SIZE OF THE HEART.

ATLANTIC CITY
OR BUST

I awoke this glorious morning knowing that today especially would be a day to celebrate—I would be putting the finishing touches on the manuscript for this book (excluding the endless editing, rereading, and fine-tuning). I just didn't know how it was going to end.

Coincidentally, the perfect ending was waiting right around the bend. Literally.

The day began with an early-morning twenty-mile bike ride from my summer home in Ocean City, New Jersey, to Atlantic City and back. I had the pleasure of being accompanied by two of my buddies, Joe "Bator" Masters and Steve "Stevie A" Ang.

On the return trip, I as the lead cyclist spotted an elderly gray-haired gentleman in biking attire thumbing a ride in our direction. Coming closer, I noticed his bicycle leaning up against the guardrail and figured he, unfortunately, must have sustained a flat tire. Since I knew that we had no repair equipment, however, there'd be no point to our stopping. Besides, it's a well-traveled road, so someone would stop to help soon. I figured a supportive wave would suffice under the circumstances.

But just at the moment when we waved a sympathetic acknowledgment, the old man yelled out: "Does anyone know how to fix a twisted chain?"

I slowed down cautiously, making sure to avoid having Bator and Stevie A crash into my rear end, and we came to a complete stop about fifty feet beyond the stranded cyclist. We backtracked carefully up the narrow two-lane highway that cuts through the marshlands between the two South Jersey islands.

Stevie A jumped in immediately with both hands, attempting to untangle the greasy chain. After a few minutes of pulling and twisting and turning and cursing, Stevie was unsuccessful. So Bator and I flipped the bike over to have a closer look.

It appeared that the chain had somehow been twisted in a way that left one long, languid kink in it. Which, of course, makes no sense. I knew from years of performing high-level magic tricks with ropes that there had to be an equal and opposite kink somewhere in the chain to counteract the one that we could see. I'm not going to reveal any magic tricks here (my magician friends would hang me with one of their ropes if I did!), but let's just say that the second, invisible, kink would enable us to release the one that we could see—the one that had stranded this poor and patient cyclist.

Bator helped me adjust the derailleur that funnels the chain through the gears of the back wheel, and we both silently agreed to give Stevie A a second chance to get even dirtier and redeem himself before either one of us snagged the bragging rights.

Sure enough, Stevie A found the second kink, we pulled the entire chain straight, and in minutes the old man was back on his bike burning calories. He left us with a hearty handshake and a promise to buy us drinks if our paths should ever cross again.

We smiled, more at how good we felt at the moment than at his generous offer of appreciation (knowing that my buddies could drink him into bankruptcy). We slapped some dirty-handed high fives with each other, saddled up, and headed home.

And now, not only did I feel great physically and mentally—fully prepared to attack the completion of this book—but I also felt great spiritually. For I already had tonight's entry in mind for my Victory Journal: "Unknotting a biker's chain of pain."

Conclusion

As I wrote in the introduction, it is my hope and intent that *Lead or Get Off the Pot!* will enable you to become a better leader, no matter what your age, your venture, or your station in life may be.

I've shared with you my seven-point system of successful leadership in seven chapters. And now I would like to leave you with a final thought, one last tool you can use in the mirror—or face-to-face with your team—to assist you on your journey from the vision to the victory celebration.

It's just a simple question that, in order to work, requires a simple, honest answer.

I remember it first being asked by my father on Thanksgiving Day more than three decades ago. I have heard it repeated over the years in a number of ways by an assortment of coaches, teachers, mentors, and caring leaders, but that first time left an indelible mark. . . .

On our drive back home from my final high school football game—which we lost in a nail-biter by one point—my father, knowing I was extremely disappointed that my last battle as a high school senior would be recorded in the annals of sports as a loss, turned to me and asked: "Was that your very best?"

Was that your very best?

It didn't matter that I was barely a starter on the team. It didn't matter that I played on only the defensive side of the field. It didn't matter how important my role was, or even *what* it was. What mattered was whether I paid the toll toward the achievement of the goal.

Was that your very best?

It's a question that you should ask all the time. And either way you answer it, if you're honest, it will steer you true.

If your performance was not your very best, but you have the guts to face the metaphorical mirror . . . well, you are guaranteed to find, deep down, a twinge of guilt and ultimately the admission: *I could have done better.* Use this hard-earned knowledge to improve the next time.

And if your performance *was* your very best, then you can rest assured that God will take care of the rest. But first, you have to ask the questions.

Do you paint your vision in vivid colors for all to see clearly and embrace? Do you invest the necessary time and effort into building a *passionate* team that can feel the fruition of your vision and goals? Do you listen with an eye to the future and preach your mission with the intensity of a never-say-die winner? Do you walk the talk every day and in every way? Is leading by the Golden Rule your rule of thumb? And do you share this path less taken with a celebratory salute to all who assist you along the journey?

Was that your very best?

It becomes the mantra of a leader . . . in every walk of life.

Change your life with these inspirational books from Pat Croce.

I Feel Great and You Will Too!
0-7432-2213-X
$14.00/$21.50 Can.

110%
0-7432-3514-2
$10.00/$16.00 Can.

Now available from Fireside Books

FIRESIDE
A Division of Simon & Schuster
A VIACOM COMPANY